ABC OF CHILD ABUSE

ABC OF CHILD ABUSE

SECOND EDITION

edited by

ROY MEADOW FRCP

Professor of Paediatrics and Child Health, St James's University Hospital, Leeds

with contributions by

FRANK BAMFORD, INGRID DAVISON, SYLVIA FRASER, CHRIS HOBBS, ALEX LEVIN,
BARBARA MITCHELS, RORY NICOL, MICHAEL PRESTON-SHOOT, RAINE ROBERTS, DAVID SKUSE,
NIGEL SPEIGHT

Published by the BMJ Publishing Group
Tavistock Square, London WC1H 9JR

First printed 1989
Second impression 1991
Second edition 1993

British Library Cataloguing Publication Data
A catalogue record for this book is available from the British Library

ISBN 0–7279–0764–6

Printed in Great Britain by Jolly & Barber Ltd, Rugby
Typesetting by Apek Typesetters, Avon House, Blackfriars Road, Nailsea, Bristol BS19 2DJ

Contents

Acknowledgements

I thank the medical illustration departments at St James's University Hospital, Leeds, Royal Victoria Infirmary, Newcastle, General Hospital, Newcastle; Mr Peter Grencist, medical photographer, Dryburn Hospital, Durham, and Dr Myles Clarke (for the illustration of lichen sclerosus).

The drawing of retinal haemorrhage is reproduced from Ludwig S, Kornberg AE. *Child Abuse, A Medical Reference.* New York: Churchill Livingstone, 1991.

The help and careful work of Mandy Jones is acknowledged with much gratitude.

EPIDEMIOLOGY

Roy Meadow

This week at least four children in Britain will die as a result of abuse or neglect. This year most departments of social services and of child health will be notified of more than 20 times as many cases of suspected child abuse as they were 10 years ago. Although some of the reports will prove to be unfounded, the common experience is that proved cases of child abuse are four or five times as common as they were a decade ago. The names of nearly 45 000 children in England are listed on child protection registers. This poses enormous burdens on staff in the health and social services and raises many problems about the lives and welfare of children in our society. Determining whether there is a true increase of child abuse or whether the figures merely reflect increased awareness rests to some extent on the definition of child abuse.

Definition

A child is considered to be abused if he or she is treated in a way that is unacceptable in a given culture at a given time. The last two clauses are important because not only are children treated differently in different countries but within a country, and even within a city, there are subcultures of behaviour and variations of opinion about what constitutes abuse of children. Moreover,

standards obviously change over the years: corporal punishment has become significantly less acceptable in Britain in the past 10 years. Looking back further there is evidence that the abuse of children by parents was considered to be culturally acceptable in Britain 100 years ago. At the time that Lord Shaftesbury was creating better conditions for children at work he was unwilling to tackle the problem of child abuse at home.

> The evils are enormous and indisputable, but they are so private, internal and domestic a character as to be beyond the reach of legislation and the subject would not, I think, be entertained in either House of Parliament.
> LORD SHAFTESBURY, 1880

In fact the first charter for children appeared in 1889, some 67 years after the introduction of legislation to protect animals.

Types of abuse

Physical abuse (non-accidental injury)—The prototype of physical abuse, "the battered baby," was rediscovered by Henry Kempe of Denver, Colorado, in 1962 and has been well publicised ever since. Physical abuse entails soft tissue injury to the skin, eyes, ears, and internal organs as well as to ligaments and bones. Burns and scalds are included. Most of this abuse is short term and violent, though it

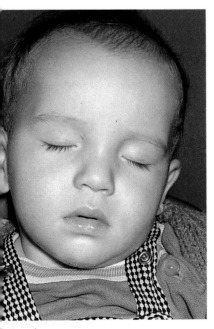

Poisoning

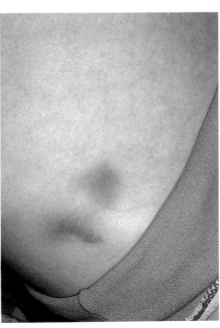

Pinching

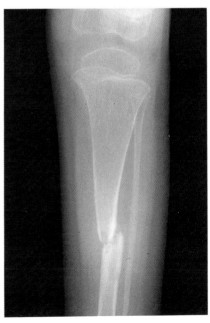

Breaking

1

Epidemiology

Punching

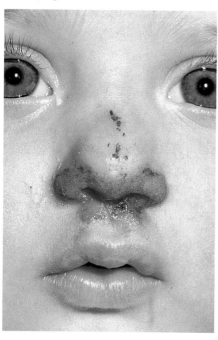

Slapping

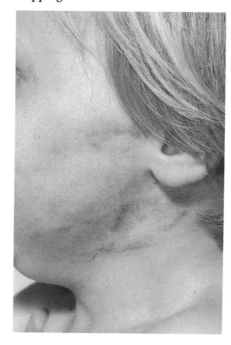

Lashing

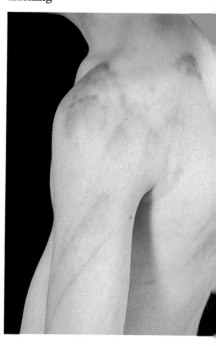

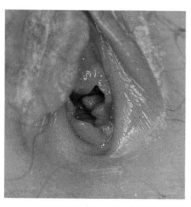

Raping

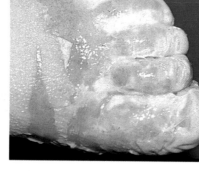

Scalding

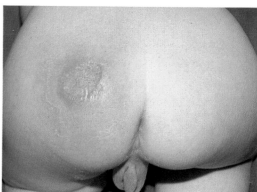

Burning

may be repetitive. There is, however, a subgroup that entails more long term deliberate injury, including poisoning and suffocation.

Neglect—This is failing to provide the love, care, food, or physical circumstances that will allow a child to grow and develop normally. Or it is exposing a child to any kind of danger.

Sexual abuse—This occurs when dependent, developmentally immature children and adolescents participate in sexual activities that they do not fully comprehend, to which they are unable to give informed consent, and that violate the social taboos of family roles. Such abuse ranges from inappropriate fondling and masturbation to intercourse and buggery. Children may also be forced to participate in producing pornographic photographs and videos, or be victims of extended family network abuse, sex rings, or ritual abuse.

Emotional abuse—This has no generally agreed definition. Some regard a child as abused if he or she has a behavioural disturbance to which the parents fail to respond appropriately in terms of modifying their behaviour or seeking professional help. Most would consider a child to be emotionally abused, however, if the child's behaviour and emotional development were severely affected by the parents' persistent neglect or rejection. Thus emotional abuse may lead to a failure to thrive and short stature in young children. Other less common forms of emotional abuse include the Munchausen syndrome by proxy, in which the parents force the child into a role of inappropriate illness.

Commonly, different types of abuse overlap with each other so a child may be being abused in several different ways either at the same time or sequentially.

Clearly, in most forms of abuse the abuser, usually the parent, may harm the child both actively and passively and by acts of both commission and omission. One parent may be active in beating the child, another just as harmful by passively failing to protect a child from the sexual advances of a cohabitant. A parent who passively fails to provide food or love for a child may indulge also in active physical assault.

2

arving

Cutting

Buggering

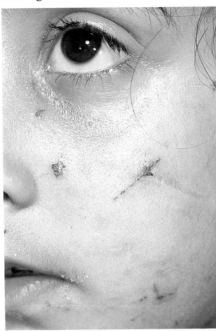
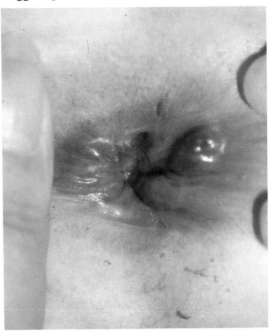

Prevalence

Four per cent of children up to the age of 12 are brought to the notice of professional agencies (social service departments or the National Society for the Prevention of Cruelty to Children) because of suspected abuse. Some of that abuse is not proved and some of it is mild, but a British survey has shown that each year at least one child per 1000 under the age of 4 years suffers severe physical abuse—for example, fractures, brain haemorrhage, severe internal injuries, or mutilation. A minimum mortality is one in 10 000 children; most people concerned with child abuse believe the mortality to be considerably higher as many cases are undetected.

The prevalence of other types of abuse is even more difficult to determine. Much depends upon how the abuse is defined and whether minor degrees of abuse are included in a study. This problem is particularly apparent in sexual abuse.

Most adults can remember an unpleasant sexual event or inappropriate approach that was made to them as a child, but if it was merely someone who indulged in indecent exposure on one occasion or fumbled about his or her clothing they probably do not consider that they have been sexually abused. Most reported instances of sexual abuse do not entail physical contact; abuse entailing physical contact, in terms of attempted or actual intercourse, is likely to be more important and certainly causes more concern. Many of the recent mass surveys have failed to distinguish between different types of abuse or to deal with the severity or repetition of the abuse. Moreover, the authors sometimes seem to forget the limitations of adults reporting past sexual experiences, particularly if they are doing so at a time of emotional upset (perhaps

Freud's writings of 80 years ago should be compulsory reading for all research workers). Home Office criminal statistics yield merely a few hundred cases a year of sexual abuse of children and grossly underrepresent the true incidence, tending more to reflect detection skills and prosecution practice. The National Society for the Prevention of Cruelty to Children reported a yearly incidence of sexual abuse in 1986 of 0·57 cases per 1000 children. This figure was based on the number of children entered on to child protection registers because of sexual abuse that year. It reflects the degree of suspicion at that time and the practices of the local authorities keeping the child abuse registers: it does not give any indication of the type or severity of the abuse.

Thus, although there is some evidence that there may have been an increase in some forms of child abuse in the past ten years, the current escalation of reported cases and identified cases is much more a matter of public awareness, better professional recognition, and an unwillingness by society to tolerate the abuse of children.

In April 1991, 45 200 children were on child protection registers in England, a rate of 4·2 children per 1000 population below the age of 18 years. About a quarter of the children on the registers were in the care of local authorities, and another 10% were subject to supervision orders. The highest rates for registration are for children under the age of 5 years, and particularly for those aged under 1 year.

Child protection registers	
Main reason for child being on register (1991)	
Grave concern	47%
Physical abuse	20%
Sexual abuse	12%
Neglect	12%
Emotional abuse	6%

Aetiology

Boys and girls are both abused. First born children are more often affected, and within a family it is common for just one of the children to be abused and the others to be free from such abuse. Young children are most at risk, partly because they are more vulnerable and partly because they cannot seek help elsewhere. Children under 2 years of age are most at risk from severe physical abuse. Death from abuse is rare after the age of 1 year.

Most abuse is by the child's parents, and it is particularly common for a parent or cohabitant who is living in the home but is not related to the child to be the abuser. Young parents are more likely to abuse than older ones. It is common for both parents to be involved with physical abuse and neglect; sex abuse is more commonly perpetrated by men, whilst poisoning, suffocation, and Munchausen syndrome by proxy abuse are usually perpetrated by the mother. Abusing parents usually do not have an identified mental illness, though many show personality traits predisposing to violent behaviour or inappropriate sexual behaviour. Child abuse is more likely in those who are socially deprived and in families without employment, but it is most important to recognise that it occurs in all layers of society.

Abuse is thought to be 20 times more likely if one of the parents was abused as a child. Though there is a strong tendency for those who were abused to abuse their own children in turn, more than a third of mothers abused as children nevertheless provide good care for their children and do not abuse them.

Awareness of the commonness of child abuse is an important step towards its recognition. The other necessary requirement is for doctors and nurses to be aware of the awful variety of ways in which children are abused. We can all understand the way in which a weary parent strikes an exasperating child but many normal people are too decent to imagine the degree of depravity, violence, cruelty, and cunning associated with child abuse. It is necessary to be aware of these wider limits because we can recognise and manage disorders only if we know about them from either experience or teaching. The chapters that follow will deal with both the common and the less common forms of child abuse.

Further reading

Creighton SJ. The incidence of child abuse and neglect. In: Browne K, Davies C, Stratton P, eds. *Early prediction and prevention of child abuse.* Chichester: Wiley, 1988.
Feldman MD, Feldman MA, Goodman JT, McGrath PJ, Pless RP, Corsini MSW, Bennett S. Is childhood sexual abuse really increasing in prevalence? An analysis of the evidence. *Pediatrics* 1991;88:29–33.
Finkelhor D, Korbin J. Child abuse as an international issue. *Child Abuse Negl* 1988;12:3–23.
Kempe CH, Silverman FN, Steele BF, Droegmuller W, Silver HK. The battered-child syndrome. *JAMA* 1962;181:17–24.
Widom CS. Sampling biases and implications for child abuse research. *Am J Orthopsychiatry* 1988;58:260–70.

NON-ACCIDENTAL INJURY

Nigel Speight

> **Child abuse is the difference between a hand on the bottom and a fist in the face.**
>
> HENRY KEMPE

Difficulty of diagnosis

The diagnosis of physical abuse (non-accidental injury) is a difficult intellectual and emotional exercise. It is one of the most difficult subjects in clinical work, needing time, experience, and emotional energy. The biggest barrier to diagnosis is the existence of emotional blocks in the minds of professionals. These can be so powerful that they prevent the diagnosis even being considered in quite obvious cases (see, for example, case 1).

All those working with children should be warned that their overwhelming impulse on confronting their first case will be to want to cover it up.

The most important step in diagnosing non-accidental injury is to force yourself to think of it in the first place.

Importance of diagnosis

Non-accidental injury is one of the most important diagnoses in clinical paediatrics as it can so vitally influence a child's future life. At worst it is a matter of life and death for the child, and short of death there may still be possible brain damage or handicap. Though high risk cases are currently in a minority, the diagnosis remains crucially important in every case. This is because non-accidental injury is often a marker for emotional abuse and deprivation that can cause progressive and possibly permanent damage to a child's developing personality. This principle is especially relevant in children of school age. In such children the risk of death may be extremely small, yet non-accidental injury in older children is almost inevitably associated with a longstanding disturbance of the parent–child relationship. For this reason non-accidental injury should never be dismissed as "overchastisement."

Non-accidental injury is not a full diagnosis, it is merely a symptom of disordered parenting. The aim of intervention is to diagnose and cure (if possible) the disordered parenting. Simply to aim at preventing death is a lowly ambition.

In some cases the occurrence of physical abuse may provide an opportunity for intervention. If this opportunity is missed there may be no further opportunity for many years.

Diagnostic features

There are no hard and fast rules and no easy answers for diagnosis. The following list constitutes seven classic "pointers" to the diagnosis. None of them is diagnostic, neither does the absence of any of them exclude the diagnosis of non-accidental injury.

(1) There is a delay in seeking medical help (or medical help is not sought at all).

(2) The story of the "accident" is vague, is lacking in detail, and may vary with each telling and from person to person. (Innocent accidents tend to have vivid accounts that ring true.)

(3) The account of the accident is not compatible with the injury observed.

(4) The parents' affect is abnormal. Normal parents are full of creative anxiety for the child. Abusing parents tend to be more

Case 1: The importance of what the child says

This 4 year old girl had been "rehabilitated" under a care order 8 months previously. She was brought to hospital with a fractured femur. Her father claimed that she had fallen down stairs, and despite the excessive bruising on her thigh and buttocks and her abject appearance no questions were asked. The next morning she told a nurse, "Daddy told Mummy he would never do it again." On further questioning the father became aggressive and had to be restrained by police from abducting the child after attempting to remove her Gallow's traction.

5

Case 2: The importance of the child's appearance

These pictures show the "before and after" effect when severe deprivation is reversed. This 3 year old boy was in fact never subjected to non-accidental injury, but many children in cases of non-accidental injury may have the same appearance. He was admitted after a genuine accident and noted to be extremely deprived. The bond between him and his mother was non-existent. (He had been admitted two years before with non-organic failure to thrive and retardation but allowed to lapse from medical follow up with no referral to social services.) In the ward he showed noticeable affection-seeking behaviour and flourished. The follow up photograph was taken six months later, while he was in foster care.

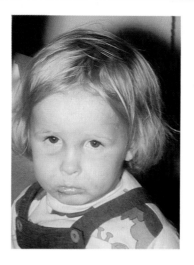 

preoccupied with their own problems—for example, how they can return home as soon as possible.

(5) The parents' behaviour gives cause for concern—for example, they soon become hostile, they rebut accusations that have not been made, and they leave before the consultant arrives.

(6) The child's appearance and his interaction with his parents are abnormal. He may look sad, withdrawn, or frightened (case 2). There may be visible evidence of failure to thrive. Full blown frozen watchfulness is a late stage and results from repetitive physical and emotional abuse over a period of time. The absence of frozen watchfulness does not exclude the diagnosis of non-accidental injury.

(7) The child may say something (case 1). Always make a point of interviewing the child (if old enough) in a safe place in private. This is one of the virtues of admission to hospital. Interviewing the child as an outpatient may fail to let the child open up as he is expecting to be returned to the custody of the abusing parent in the near future.

Characteristic patterns of injury

Some forms of injury are by their nature virtually diagnostic of non-accidental injury.

These include finger tip bruising, especially when it is multiple (cases 3 and 4); adult human bite marks; cigarette burns; lash marks (case 5); and torn frenulum. In addition, unexplained subdural haematomata and retinal haemorrhages (see pages 15 and 18) are highly suggestive of non-accidental injury.

How to approach a case of suspected non-accidental injury

Approach the parents as you would in any other clinical situation. Introduce yourself, shake hands, and proceed logically through the history, examination, provisional diagnosis, and decision making. Look at the "whole child," including other medical problems, and take a social history to form a picture of the family background. Look at the child's growth and development, since a degree of failure to thrive and impaired development due to neglect or emotional deprivation commonly coexist with physical abuse. Proper documentation at this stage will allow estimates of subsequent "catch up" growth and development to be made.

Try to avoid jumping to conclusions too soon. Proceed slowly and deliberately, keeping your mind open as long as possible. Avoid confrontation or accusing parents at this stage (although confrontation does have a part to

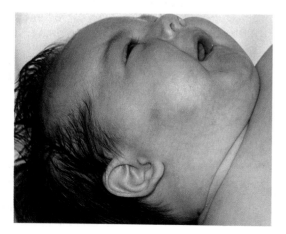

Case 3: Finger tip bruising and fractured ribs

This 4 month old baby was noted to have two bruises on the cheek highly suggestive of finger tip bruising from forceful gripping. A skeletal survey showed two healing rib fractures caused by an episode 4 to 8 weeks previously.

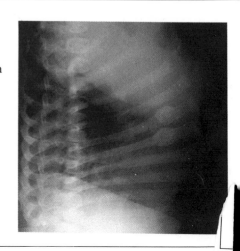

play in management once the diagnosis of abuse is definite).

Note keeping

The importance of good note keeping cannot be overemphasised, both for referring doctors and paediatricians. Discrepancies between first and subsequent accounts of the "accident" can be important when information is shared at a case conference, but need to be backed up by notes taken contemporaneously. Any medical notes may be scrutinized at a later date in a court of law, therefore loose or derogatory phraseology is best avoided.

Ideally all conversations with parents or caretakers should be recorded in full, and it is wise to have another member of staff present on each occasion as a precaution against subsequent complaints by the parents.

Bruises and other injuries should be described verbally and recorded diagrammatically using body charts. In addition, colour photographs should be taken whenever possible as they are such a vivid and accurate record of what has happened. Photographs can be very helpful in making the injuries real for case conference members, and

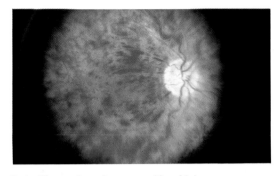

Retinal haemorrhage from non-accidental injury

are valuable as evidence in court. Subsequently they may enable a social worker to continue to confront parents with the reality of the abuse if they are attempting to minimize it.

Ageing of bruises

Bruises of different ages are a common feature of abuse and it is important to be able to give some estimate of the age of individual bruises, without attempting to be too exact. The following is a rough guide for superficial bruises.

- <24 hours   red/purple
- 12–48 hours   purplish blue
- 48–72 hours   brown
- >72 hours   yellow.

Bruises to avascular areas (for example, pinna of ear) or deep bruises may evolve at a slower rate than the above.

Investigations

When non-accidental bruising is suspected, blood tests should be performed to exclude medical causes for excessive bruising. These tests should include full blood count, clotting screen, and platelet function tests. Even when the case is obviously one of abuse the tests should be performed in case they are needed to support the diagnosis in future court proceedings.

Just occasionally, these tests will reveal a completely unexpected medical problem—for example, leukaemia or thrombocytopenia. Other medical causes of innocent bruising include cellulitis caused by *Haemophilus influenzae*, or an apparent black eye from orbital deposits in neuroblastoma.

Skeletal survey should be performed in most infants and may reveal crucial evidence of previous bony injuries (see case 3). Repeat skeletal survey can be very useful in the follow up assessment of acute injuries as it may reveal previously unsuspected rib fractures and subperiosteal calcification of long bones in infants whose first skeletal survey was normal. It is much less appropriate in older children and should be used only in selected cases.

In all cases the local child protection register should be checked (usually via the duty social worker) to see if the child, or anyone else in the family, has been considered to be at risk or a source of concern to social services previously.

Case 4: Finger tip bruising

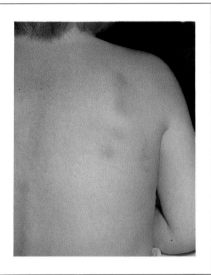

This 2 year old boy was admitted with a fractured tibia, bruising to the face, and classic finger tip bruising over the right scapula.

Case 5: Lash marks

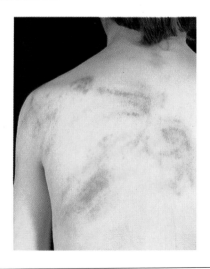

This 10 year old girl was whipped with a belt by her depressed father. The linear nature of the marks is seen, together with a tramlining effect, in which the point of impact is white and the adjoining skin shows bruising caused by capillaries that have been broken by blood being forced into them.

Non-accidental injury

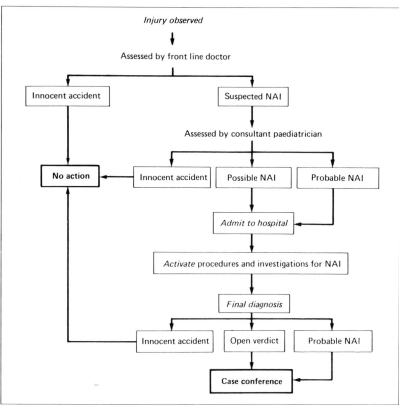

Flow chart for referral of cases of suspected non-accidental injury (NAI)

Hospital admission

It can be seen that hospital admission offers many advantages in the assessment, documentation, and investigation of suspected non-accidental injury. In obvious cases it allows a breathing space for social services in their decision making, as the child is in a place of safety. In doubtful cases, it gives the paediatrician time to get the diagnosis right (see flow chart). It can also give valuable information from direct observation of parent-child interaction and parental visiting pattern.

Referral pathway

The diagnosis of non-accidental injury is a two tier exercise. The doctor on the front line (general practitioner, senior house officer in the accident and emergency department, or school doctor) is responsible for identifying children with suspected physical abuse and referring them to a consultant paediatrician for definitive diagnosis.

Role of front line doctors

Doctors on the front line must realise and accept the limits of their responsibility. They do not have to make a definitive diagnosis and should have a comparatively low threshold of referral. It should be accepted that some children with innocent injuries will be referred. If all of the children referred turn out to have been physically abused the threshold for referral is almost certainly too high.

Front line doctors should not feel guilt about referring children with suspected non-accidental injury to a paediatrician. They are not accusing either parent; they are simply asking for a second opinion on an important and difficult diagnosis. The fact that the child is being referred because of suspected non-accidental injury should be conveyed to the parents in a neutral and matter of fact way. It is not in the interests of children or parents for child abuse to be covered up. To do so leaves the parents at greater risk of inflicting more severe injuries next time, being imprisoned for causing more severe injuries, and losing long term custody of their children. Early intervention may help to prevent these events.

It is the duty of front line doctors to refer all children with suspected non-accidental injury. Failing to do so is a form of professional negligence. In the United States failing to report suspected child abuse is a federal offence punishable by imprisonment.

Role of the consultant paediatrician

It is vital to the interests of the child, the parents, and all the professionals concerned that the paediatrician reaches a correct and definite diagnosis in as many cases as possible (This duty should not be delegated to junior staff.) If the paediatrician sits on the fence he or she will not only be in an uncomfortable position but also be doing a disservice to the child and the parents. If the paediatrician finds it impossible to decide initially he or she should admit the child to hospital while investigations continue. Few cases are uncertain after a thorough multidisciplinary investigation. The paediatrician should remember that he or she is being asked to commit himself or herself only on the balance of probabilities—not beyond all reasonable doubt. If the paediatrician genuinely cannot decide between non-accidental injury and an innocent injury, he or she should return an open verdict and decisions should be guided by the psychosocial assessment.

Further reading

Wilson EF. Estimation of the age of cutaneous contusions in child abuse. *Paediatrics* 1977;**60**:750–2.

FRACTURES

Chris Hobbs

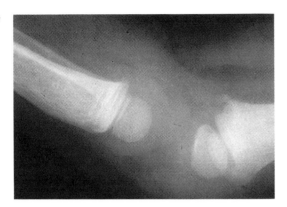

Metaphyseal (corner) fracture of lower end of femur in a child of 15 months who was swung by the legs and hit head against a wall

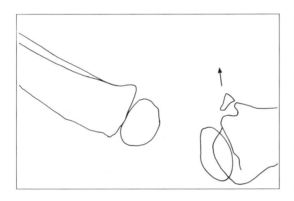

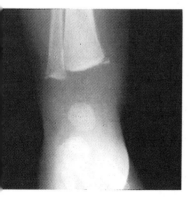

Distal metaphyseal chip fractures of lower end of tibia and fibula in abused infant

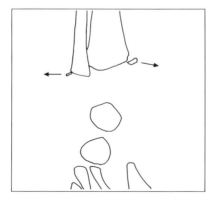

under 3 years old and they sustained most of the fractures (94%). In contrast, accidental fractures occur more commonly in children of school age.

The proportion of children presenting to hospital with fractures resulting from physical abuse rises to a maximum during the first year of life, when it may be as high as a half. A great deal of suspicion is required at this age. Most accidental fractures in infants and toddlers result from falls, although fractures are uncommon in falls of under a metre.

As early detection improves the proportion of children with fractures who are identified as having been physically abused falls from 50% to 10% or less. Most children with serious injury have suffered minor injury or shown other signs of abuse that have not been recognised or acted on by professionals in contact with the child.

Detecting fractures due to physical abuse

Children whose fractures are the result of an accident present crying excessively, with swelling or bruising, and are reluctant to use the affected part—for example, to put weight on a leg.

Some fractures caused by physical abuse are detected only by radiology because the fracture may be old, the physical signs having regressed; the site may be hidden—for example, the ribs, pelvis, or skull—and the parents will not have drawn attention to the possibility of injury.

Important patterns

Six important patterns are seen in fractures caused by physical abuse.

(1) A single fracture with multiple bruises.

(2) Multiple fractures in different stages of healing, possibly with no bruises or soft tissue injuries.

(3) Metaphyseal-epiphyseal injuries which are often multiple.

(4) Rib fractures.

(5) The formation of new periosteal bone.

(6) A skull fracture in association with intracranial injury.

As with all forms of physical abuse a careful history and examination and appraisal of the family potential for child abuse provides the framework for diagnosis.

Skeletal survey

The radiographic survey of the child's

Fractures are among the most serious injuries sustained after physical abuse. They may occur in almost any bone and may be single or multiple, clinically obvious or occult and detectable only by radiography.

Prevalence

In one study of physically abused children more than half of the children (58%) were

Fractures

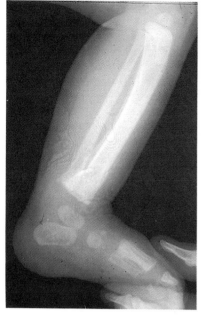

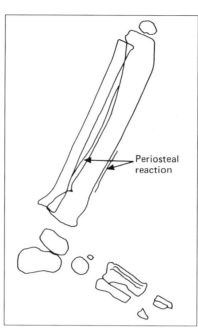

Periosteal reaction

Distal non-displaced fracture of lower shafts of tibia and fibula in abused child of 6 months, with evidence of periosteal reaction along tibial shafts. Fracture is probably 10–14 days old. Other injuries included multiple rib and complex skull fractures

skeleton must be complete. Babygrams (the whole baby in one radiograph) are generally unacceptable. Radionuclide bone scanning has a lower radiation dose and is generally more sensitive in detecting abnormalities (for example, rib fractures). It cannot detect healed injuries nor assess healing stages and may miss metaphyseal lesions around normally "hot" epiphyseal growth plates. Conventional radiography provides a high level of specificity and most injuries can be determined in this way.

Consider skeletal survey

- When injury or history suggest physical abuse

- In all children less than 24 months old

- In older children with severe bruising

- For localised pain, limp, or reluctance to use arm or leg

- When history of skeletal injury present

- In children dying in unusual or suspicious circumstances

Specificity of radiological findings

No lesion is absolutely pathognomic of physical abuse but some carry higher specificity than others.

High specificity findings are metaphyseal or epiphyseal fractures, or both (corner and bucket handle fractures, chip fractures); rib fractures; multiple or wide complex skull fractures, or both; scapular and sternal fractures, which are uncommon; multiple fractures; fractures of different ages; and unpresented fractures.

Low specificity findings are single fractures; linear, narrow parietal skull fractures; fractures in the shafts of long bones; and clavicular fractures.

Rib fractures

Rib fractures are usually occult and detect by radiography or radionuclide bone scanning. In infancy the ribs are very pliable and unless there is bone disease severe trauma can be implied.

Cardiopulmonary resuscitation is not responsible in this age group and unless an unusual history of direct thoracic trauma is given, abuse is extremely likely.

The fractures, frequently multiple, bilateral and posterior, are thought to follow thoracic compression and distortion of the rib cage during shaking episodes, or from kicks or blows in older children.

Metaphyseal and epiphyseal fractures

Metaphyseal and epiphyseal fractures are the classic injuries of physical abuse. Fragments of bone become separated from the ends of long bones either as a chip or as a whole plate. Such injuries arise from acceleration and deceleration as the infant is shaken by the body, arms, or legs. The forces of pulling and twisting applied to the weak metaphyseal area of bone disrupt a fine layer of new trabecular bone close to the junction with cartilage. In epiphyseal lesions the injury occurs in the zone of hypertrophic cartilage with few radiological signs initially. The usual sites are the knee, wrist, elbow, and ankle. Metaphyseal lesions appear to cause little pain, tenderness, or swelling and heal without callus formation.

Fractures of the shafts of long bones

In assessing these injuries knowledge of the claimed and likely mechanism of production

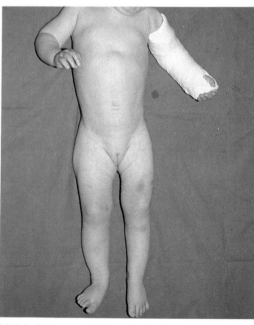

Mid-shaft fracture of radius and ulna in 14 month old girl with old bruising to her thigh and failure to thrive. Fracture in itself carries little specificity for physical abuse, but bruising and growth chart (overleaf) greatly increase likelihood of physical abuse. Cohabiting boyfriend of girl's mother admitted swinging child by arm

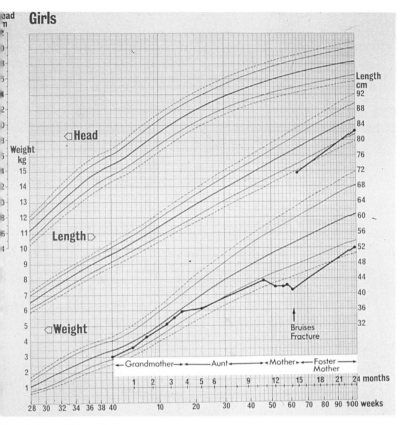

Girls

Growth chart of 14 month old girl with fractured tibia and fibula in case described on previous page. Pattern of failure to thrive developed from age of 4 months, when care was transferred to an aunt, and worsened when natural mother took over care at about 12 months. Catch up in length and weight were seen in foster mother's care. Children may react to changes in carer by developing behavioural difficulties, often centred on feeding, which may trigger violent responses from parents

may be useful: transverse fractures—from angulation including from a direct blow; oblique transverse from angulation or bending with axial loading (compression); spiral from axial twists with or without axial loading; and oblique from angulation, axial twisting with axial loading.

Abuse injuries commonly arise when a limb is grasped, twisted, pulled, or used as a handle to swing or shake the child.

Certain fractures are commoner in

abuse—for example, spiral humeral, femoral in infancy (up to 80% abuse), lateral clavicular, and small bones of hands and feet.

In these relatively common and usually clinically obvious injuries, however, a careful assessment of the history will assist in the recognition of abuse.

Spinal injury

Spinal injury in physical abuse usually results from hyperflexion-extension injury with damage to several consecutive levels. Defects in the lucency of the anterior superior edges of the vertebral bodies, often in the lower thoracic and upper lumbar regions, with narrowed disc spaces are characteristic. Multiple spinous process fractures are also described. Spinal cord injury may follow dislocation or subluxation.

Formation of new periosteal bone

Injury to an infant's developing long bone often results in subperiosteal haemorrhage, which raises the periosteum from the shaft while maintaining its firm attachment to the epiphysis. This process usually takes 10–14 days to appear, and radiography may yield negative results initially. The finding may also point to an underlying fracture that is not easily visualised.

Such injuries probably arise when arms and legs are grabbed, pulled, or used as a handle for shaking the child. Trauma must be distinguished from other causes—namely, infection, Caffey's disease, vitamin A intoxication, leukaemia, and certain drugs—but all of these are far less common than physical abuse.

Dating fractures

Fracture dating is of obvious medicolegal importance. The table sets out peak times, although the earliest changes are sometimes seen a few days before this.

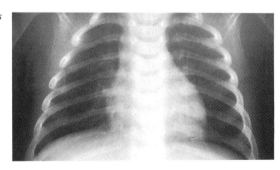

Posterior healing rib fractures of left sixth, seventh, and eighth ribs behind cardiac shadow in abused infant. Presence of callus and unclear fracture line suggests fractures are at least two weeks old

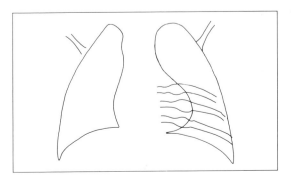

Resolution of soft tissue change	4–10 days
Periosteal new bone formation (earliest sign)	10–14 days
Loss of fracture line definition	14–21 days
Soft callus	14–21 days
Hard callus	21–42 days
Remodelling	1 year

From: Kleinman PK. *Diagnostic imaging of child abuse.* Baltimore: Williams and Wilkins, 1987.

The following should be noted:

● A fracture without periosteal new bone formation is usually less than 7–10 days old and seldom 20 days old
● A fracture with definite but slight periosteal new bone formation could be as recent as 4–7 days

Fractures

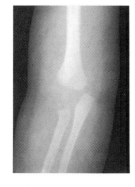
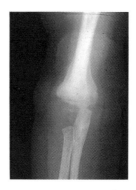
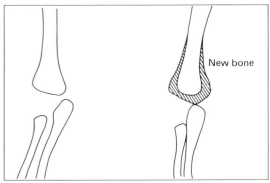

New bone

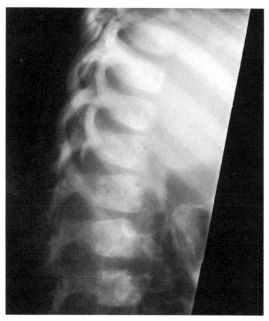
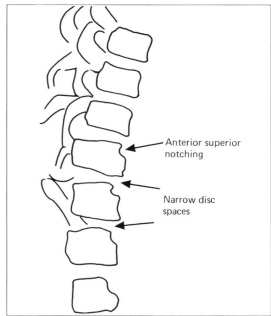

Anterior superior notching

Narrow disc spaces

● A 20 day old fracture will always have well defined periosteal reaction and typically soft callus

● A fracture with well developed periosteal new bone formation or callus is more than 14 days old.

Injury to the same (untreated) fracture may prolong healing and callus and fresh refracture may coexist.

Differential diagnosis of fractures

Child abuse is common. Non-traumatic causes of fracture or pseudofracture vary from uncommon to extremely rare. A balanced perspective is required if children's interests are to be preserved. Courts for the protection of children require probability rather than certainty in evidence.

Normal variants

The formation of new periosteal bone in infants and unusual suture lines in a skull radiograph could be normal variants.

Birth trauma

During breech deliveries the clavicle and humerus are often broken. If, however, callus is absent two weeks after birth the fracture did not occur during delivery.

Bone disease

Osteogenesis imperfecta—This inherited connective tissue disorder with abnormal collagen is occasionally confused with abuse as fractures are a major feature. There are a number of other features: bone fragility and osteoporosis; ligamentous laxity; skin fragility; blue sclera; dentinogenesis imperfecta; and presenile hearing loss.

In addition, a positive family history and wormian skull bones are features present in many cases. The condition is complex with four clinical types (I–IV), of which the rare IV is said occasionally to present clinically with little other than a fracture. This has been the basis of defence cases, although the incidence of this scenario has been estimated to lie between one in one million and one in three million births.

Copper deficiency—With osteogenesis imperfecta fractures should not suddenly cease when the child is removed to a safe environment, as they do in the case of abuse. Copper deficiency has been postulated as an explanation for temporary brittle bones in some cases of multiple fractures in infancy. Copper functions in various enzyme systems, deficiency resulting in sideroblastic anaemia, neutropenia, abnormal bones radiologically, hypotonia, and developmental retardation.

Bone abnormalities include osteoporosis, frayed and cup shaped metaphyses, and metaphyseal sickle shaped spurs, with changes distributed symmetrically throughout the skeleton. The condition occurs in low birth weight preterm infants, after prolonged total parenteral nutrition, after feeding milk deficient in copper (for example, doorstep milk), in malnutrition or malabsorption. The condition with fractures is rare. Skull and rib fractures have not been described. The plasma copper concentration is low.

Other conditions—These include prematurity (rickets), which may cause periosteal new bone formation and epiphyseal changes, which could be confused with abuse, or pathological fracture; scurvy; vitamin A intoxication; congenital syphilis; osteomyelitis; and neuropathic disorders.

Expert radiological, paediatric, and biochemical help may be required in occasional cases. The presence of a normal skeleton radiologically is strongly against the diagnosis of genetic, metabolic, or bone disease.

Further reading
Haller JO, Kleinman PK, Merten DF *et al*. Diagnostic imaging of child abuse. *Pediatrics* 1991;**87**:262–4.
Kleinman PK. *Diagnostic imaging of child abuse*. Baltimore: Williams and Wilkins, 1987.
Shaw JCL. Copper deficiency and non-accidental injury. *Arch Dis Child* 1988;**63**:448–55.
Silverman FN. Radiology and other imaging procedures. In: Helfer RE, Kempe RS, eds. *The battered child*. 4th ed. Chicago: University of Chicago Press, 1987:214
Taitz LS. Child abuse and osteogenesis imperfecta. *Br Med J* 1987;**295**:1082–3.
Thomas SA, Rosenfield NS, Leventhal JM, Markowitz RI. Long-bone fractures in young children: distinguishing accidental injuries from child abuse. *Pediatrics* 1991;**88**:471–6.
Warlock P, Stower M, Barbor P. Patterns of fractures in accidental and non-accidental injury in children: a comparative study. *Br Med J* 1986;**293**:100–2.

HEAD INJURIES

Chris Hobbs

Head injury is the major cause of fatal outcome after physical abuse. The head is the commonest target for assault in the young child. In the first year of life 95% of serious intracranial injury is the result of abuse.

Two major categories of head injury described are: focal from impacts (punches, hitting the head from throwing or swinging the child on to or against an object or surface), and diffuse injury from acceleration–deceleration phenomena (shaking). A combination of the two is thought to account for many of the most serious injuries (the shaken-impact syndrome).

Between 40% and 70% of battered children have injury of some form to the face or head. These include bruises to the face or scalp;

traumatic alopecia and subgaleal haematoma; skull or facial fracture, or both; subdural and subarachnoid haemorrhage; cerebral contusion including diffuse axonal injury; intracerebral haemorrhage; and oedema. If the child survives permanent physical and mental handicap may result.

Detecting head injuries due to physical abuse

When an infant rolls off a changing table, hospital trolley, cot, or bed, even on to a hard floor, serious injury rarely occurs. In one study 80% of infants escaped without any finding of injury whatsoever. The other 20% had a single cut, lump, or bruise. Skull fractures were found in 1%, and these were single and linear.

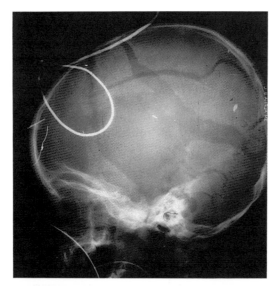
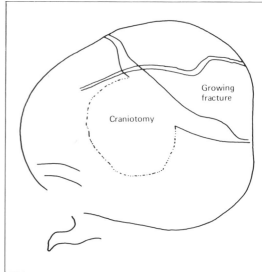

Extensive bilateral parietal fractures, which are wide and growing. Large lucent area represents surgical evacuation of large haematoma before 15 month old child died. Head was injured when the child was swung by the leg against a wall

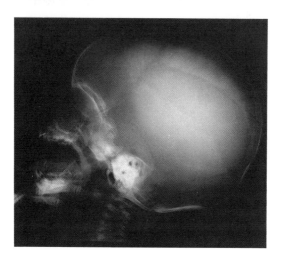
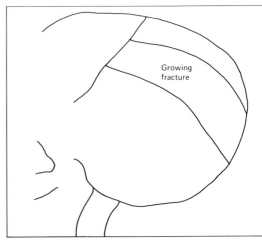

Growing fracture of parietal bone in 6 week old abused child. Father claimed to have dropped child, but old rib fractures and intracranial injury were inconsistent with history

Manifestations of skull fractures

Child usually said to have fallen or banged head—for example, on door—or history may be absent

	Accident	Physical abuse
Type	Single linear	Multiple, complex, branched
Maximum fracture width	Hairline, narrow, 1–2 mm	Wide, growing, 3 mm or more
Site	Parietal One bone only	Occipital, highly specific Bilateral, parietal More than one bone affected
Depressed	Localised with clear history of fall on to sharp object	As part of complex fracture, extensive or multiple depressed areas
Associated intracranial injury	Unusual except after severe falls (2–3 m or more). Extradural haemorrhage uncommon but serious complication of simple fracture	Subdural haemorrhage, cerebral contusion, intracerebral haemorrhage, and cerebral oedema common

If an infant presents with a cranial swelling a day or two after a minor head injury and has a hairline parietal single linear fracture the cause is usually innocent provided that other injuries are not present

An equal number had a fracture at another site, of which the clavicle and humerus were the most common. No child sustained a subdural haematoma or life threatening condition. Falls from greater heights (between 1 and 2 m), as, for example, from a standing adult's shoulder, are more likely to result in a single linear parietal hairline fracture of the skull, and the infant may be irritable, vomit, or refuse a feed. Serious intracranial injury is extremely unlikely.

Even in more serious falls from heights in excess of 2 m or down stairs where a fracture may show one or two features of abuse (table), serious intracranial injury is unusual. Occasionally, however, extradural haemorrhage can, if unrecognised and untreated, be fatal irrespective of the presence or absence of an underlying cerebral injury.

The force entailed in physical abuse—for example, in swinging the child, in violent uncontrolled shaking, and in hitting the child's head with a fist or foot or against a wall—is so much greater that the pattern of injury is different and serious intracranial injury results. Accidental intracranial injury in infancy is rare.

Scalp injury

The presence of injury to the scalp is often shown by a swelling, which can reach considerable size. This may represent bruising to the scalp tissues; if there is a fracture a subgaleal haematoma forms, into which much blood may be lost. Subgaleal haematoma also results from hair pulling as, for example, when a child is picked up by the hair. The swelling is diffuse and boggy and there are broken hairs with occasionally petechiae at the roots. There are no signs of scalp disease, such as loose hairs or scaling, which helps differentiate it from other forms of alopecia.

Skull fractures

Fractures indicate blunt impact injuries. Their reliable detection in a radiograph requires a radiologist or doctor experienced in differentiating usual and unusual suture lines in infants, which may be difficult. Swelling over the area helps, but the radiograph needs to be examined with bright light illumination.

The radiograph must be interpreted alongside the history. When there is a history of a minor fall, as is usually the case in infants and toddlers during the first two years, significant differences exist between the patterns of fracture after abuse and those after an accident. These are summarised in the table.

After abuse fractures tend to be extensive, multiple, complex or branched, depressed, wide, separated, and growing, and to cross individual suture lines, thereby affecting many individual skull bones. Whereas in accidents the parietal bone alone is usually affected by a single narrow linear fracture, in abuse other bones, notably the thick occipital bone and the base of the skull, are more likely to be fractured. Indeed, a fracture of the occipital bone should carry a high suspicion of abuse.

Growing fractures are not generally well known among doctors. These uncommon fractures occur only in infancy and entail a dural tear and brain injury beneath the facture, which subsequently enlarges to form a cranial defect. Once a fracture reaches 0·5 cm in width in a radiograph it should be carefully followed for further growth. Such fractures seem to occur after a more severe blow to the head and are therefore more likely to be associated with abuse. Surgical treatment may be required to repair the defect.

Subdural haematoma

Subdural haematomas arise in over half of cases without the presence of a skull fracture. For a while they were termed "spontaneous subdural haematomas" until it was recognised that the infants had been abused. The evidence points to violent shaking disrupting bridging cerebral veins with bleeding into the subdural space, often over a wide area bilaterally.

In some cases the only additional evidence is the presence of retinal haemorrhages and there may be no bruising or other injury to the baby. These babies have been shaken violently, usually to stop them crying. Bouncing a baby up and down on a knee or an accidental head injury resulting in a simple

Head injuries

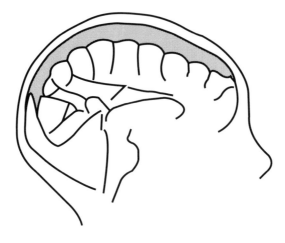

fracture does not result in subdural haematomas.

Subdural haematomas arising after birth trauma produce signs and symptoms soon after delivery and should not lead to confusion. The concept of a chronic subdural haematoma after birth trauma is extremely dubious.

Children who develop irritability, vomiting, decreasing levels of consciousness, and irregular breathing or apnoea shortly after an alleged trivial head injury have probably been abused. Parents may admit to shaking the child mildly because "he didn't look too good" or "stopped breathing." In reality the child has been violently shaken. The diagnosis, once thought of, is most easily confirmed by computed tomography, but this can occasionally miss a difficult case.

Retinal haemorrhages

These are an important finding in non-accidental injury and are discussed in detail on pages 18–19.

Cerebral contusion, haemorrhage, and oedema

Cerebral contusion, haemorrhage, and oedema are responsible for many of the deaths and long term disability resulting from physical abuse. Areas of cerebral disruption, haemorrhage, and oedema are scattered throughout the brain, which swells, leading to a short term rise in intracranial pressure. Surgery is rarely helpful.

If the child survives chronic disability is a real possibility. In one study Buchanan and Oliver estimated that between 3% and 11% of children residing in hospitals for the retarded were handicapped as a result of violent abuse. They described seizures and post-traumatic

hydrocephalus, damage to visual pathways, and cerebral infarction leading to atrophy and microcephaly.

Diagnosis of intracranial injury

When there is neither history of trauma nor obvious external signs of significant injury to the child, diagnosis may be difficult. A history of a minor household accident (for example, the child rolled off a settee or fell out of a baby bouncer) may be offered. The presentation may be with fits, unconsciousness, lethargy, and apnoea, and there may be delay in presenting the child for medical treatment.

Initially meningitis, encephalitis, infection, and toxic or metabolic disease may be considered the most likely diagnosis. Useful physical signs include a bulging fontanelle, low packed cell volume (indicating earlier injury), increasing head circumference, retinal haemorrhages, and torn frenulum.

Investigations

Lumbar puncture—May be bloody.

Skeletal survey (skull radiograph)—Look for fractures, widening of the cranial sutures.

Computed tomography—This is the examination of choice and is superior to magnetic resonance imaging in the acute stage for detecting subarachnoid haemorrhage, and will also detect cerebral oedema and subdural haemorrhage. Both subarachnoid and subdural haemorrhage are thought to arise from disrupted bridging veins between the cortex and dural sinuses, with blood tracking into the interhemispheric fissure—this is well detected by computed tomography.

Magnetic resonance imaging—This is superior to computed tomography in detecting subdural haemorrhage as well as posterior fossa intraparenchymal injuries. Non-haemorrhagic white matter contusions and shearing injuries are also better shown, and dating of extracerebral fluid collections is enhanced. Also, the pictures are more impressive in court. It is important that T1 and T2 weighted sequences are used.

Cranial sonography—This is less sensitive than computed tomography.

Further reading

Billmire ME, Myers PA. Serious head injury in infants: accident or abuse? *Pediatrics* 1985;75:340–2.
Helfer RE, Slovis TL, Black M. Injuries resulting when small children fall out of bed. *Pediatrics* 1977;60:533–5.
Hobbs CJ. Skull fracture and the diagnosis of abuse. *Arch Dis Child* 1984;59:246–52.
Kleinman PK. Head trauma. In *Diagnostic imaging in child abuse*. Baltimore: Williams and Wilkins, 1987. Chapter 8.
Sato Y *et al.* Head injury in child abuse: evaluation with MR imaging. *Pediatric Radiol* 1989;173:653–7.

OPHTHALMIC PRESENTATIONS

Alex Levin

Virtually any ocular injury may be the result of child abuse. Ocular injury is the presenting sign of physical child abuse in four to six per cent of child abuse cases. Medical non-compliance and neglect can also result in permanent visual loss. Sexual abuse may be the route of transmission of a sexually transmitted disease to the eyes. Abused children may also develop functional symptoms such as blinking, unusual visual phenomena, or non-organic visual loss. Some people may consider the diagnosis of emotional abuse when parents or other adult caretakers allow children to view inappropriate materials, such as pornography or adult sexual behaviour.

Detection of ocular manifestations

Whenever a child less than 4 years old is suspected of being a victim of physical abuse, complete eye examination, including dilatation of the pupil for retinal examination by an ophthalmologist, is essential. Examination using only a direct ophthalmoscope should not replace complete retinal examination, which can be accomplished only with the ophthalmologist's indirect (head mounted) ophthalmoscope. With indirect ophthalmoscopy retinal haemorrhages or other changes may be seen in the peripheral retina, which cannot be viewed with the direct ophthalmoscope. These findings, including peripheral retinal tears, may have particular importance in identifying the abused child. However, use of the direct ophthalmoscope by the primary care or emergency doctor can be a useful screening test. The pupils should be dilated with one drop of phenylephrine 2·5% and cyclopentolate 1% (except in premature infants, when cyclopentolate 0·5% is preferred). These drops may be repeated after 20 minutes if the pupils are not adequately fixed and dilated. If there is concern about using pupillary reactivity to monitor a child's neurological status, the cyclopentolate (duration of mydriasis up to one day) may be omitted. With phenylephrine alone pupillary reactivity should return in four to six hours. Despite the value of a positive direct ophthalmoscope examination, the absence of abnormalities, in particular retinal haemorrhages, does not obviate the need for consultation with an ophthalmologist. This is particularly true when shaking injuries are suspected. If an ophthalmologist is readily available it is best to forego pupillary dilatation unless he or she specifically requests it as he or she may wish to examine the child initially before pupillary dilation.

Child abuse must be in the differential diagnosis when evaluating any eye injury. There are a number of ocular abnormalities which, when found, might suggest that trauma has occurred, even when a history to the contrary is given.

Whenever a child less than 4 years old dies suddenly for no apparent reason, gross and histological examination of the eyeballs should be included as part of the necropsy. Before removal of the eyeballs, an ophthalmologist, if available, may be asked to examine the child's retinas in situ to look for abnormalities such as retinal haemorrhages. Regardless of the result of the ophthalmologist's evaluation, both eyeballs should be removed, preferably along

Ocular indicators of trauma

	Result of injury	Comment
Eyelids	Laceration,* ecchymosis	Unilateral/bilateral ecchymosis may follow forehead trauma
Eyeball	Ruptured globe* (corneal/scleral laceration)	
Conjunctiva	Subconjunctival haemorrhage	Also from suffocation/ strangle or abdominal or chest trauma
	Chemical burns	
Cornea	Scars	Especially bilateral acquired
Anterior chamber	Hyphema	
Lens	Cataract	Especially if unilateral
	Dislocated lens	Especially if unilateral
Vitreous	Haemorrhage	
	Detached vitreous base*	
Retina	Haemorrhage, contusion* (Berlin's oedema, commotio retinae)	
	Retinal detachment	Especially if bilateral

* Pathognomic for trauma.

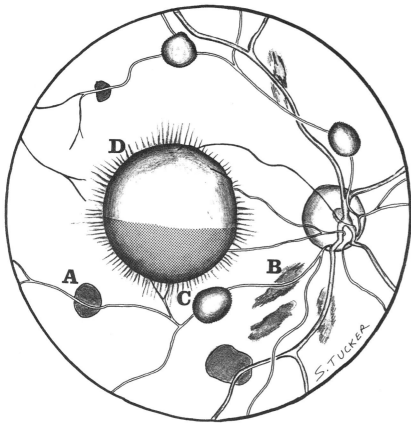

A Intraretinal haemorrhage—blood vessel passes into and through haemorrhage. B Superficial flame shaped haemorrhage. C Preretinal haemorrhage—blood vessel obscured. D Traumatic retinoschisis

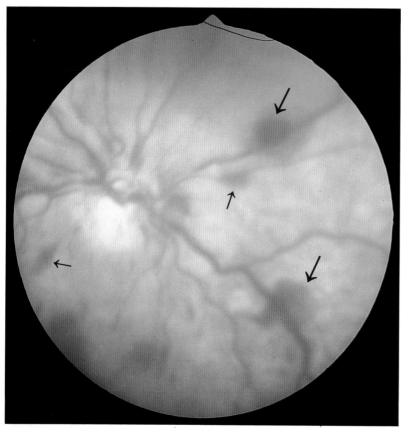

Retinal haemorrhages in an abused child. Small arrows indicate superficial flame shaped haemorrhages. Large arrows indicate "blot" intraretinal haemorrhages. No traumatic retinoschisis is seen in this patient

with the entire orbital contents from a combined anterior and intracranial approach after removal of the brain. After fixation these tissues should be sectioned *en bloc*. Any gross or histological abnormalities should be photographed. If the pathologist is unable to remove the orbital tissues with the eyeball, then the entire globe, along with a long segment of optic nerve, should be removed from an anterior approach.

Consultation with an ophthalmologist may also be helpful in the following circumstances: conjunctivitis in a case of alleged child sexual abuse; suspected Munchausen syndrome by proxy with ocular signs or symptoms; the neglected child; and the abused child with visual complaints.

Retinal haemorrhages

Retinal haemorrhages are one of the cardinal signs of the shaken baby syndrome, occurring in about 80% of cases. These haemorrhages may occur in front of, within, or under the retina. They are usually bilateral. The exact mechanism by which they occur in the shaken infant is not clearly understood. Increased intracranial pressure; subdural or subarachnoid haemorrhage, or both; chest compression by the perpetrator's hand; and direct shaking injury to the retina or optic nerve may play a part. The intracranial approach to removal of the entire orbital contents, as described above, is designed to identify injury to the retina or optic nerve. Retinal haemorrhages in children less than 4 years of age are virtually never caused by cardiopulmonary resuscitation with chest compressions or accidental head trauma. I am aware of only one convincing report of retinal haemorrhages secondary to resuscitation without other risk factors being present. These haemorrhages were few in number and confined to the posterior aspect of the retina around the optic nerve, unlike the retinal haemorrhages of the shaken baby, which tend to be distributed diffusely throughout the retina. Severe life threatening accidental head trauma (for example, that sustained in a road traffic accident), may, rarely, cause a small number of retinal haemorrhages in the posterior aspect of the retina. The type of accidental injury that would result in this clinical picture has an obvious history, eliminating any concern about child abuse.

Other systemic conditions can cause retinal haemorrhages in young children. They include acute hypertension, fulminant meningitis, vasculitis, sepsis, endocarditis, coagulopathy, leukaemia and cyanotic congenital heart disease. Fortunately, these entities are usually easy to recognise from the history, a good physical examination, a complete blood count, and basic coagulation studies. Retinal haemorrhages may also be seen after normal birth. Flame haemorrhages resolve in less than two weeks after birth. Large intraretinal dot/ blot haemorrhages may, rarely, persist for up to six weeks. Diabetes mellitus and haemoglobinopathies such as sickle cell anaemia do not cause retinal haemorrhages in the shaken baby syndrome age group.

Traumatic retinoschisis is a form of retinal injury that may be virtually pathognomic of shaking injury. Owing to concomitant shaking of the vitreous gel within the eyeball the retinal layers are split apart to cause a dome shaped cavity, which may be partially or completely filled with blood. Some observers have described similar retinal abnormalities as subhyaloid haemorrhage—a collection of blood between the retina and vitreous gel. I believe this term may have been applied incorrectly in some cases as the clinical appearance of sybhyaloid haemorrhage may be indistinguishable from superficial traumatic retinoschisis, an entity which only recently has been confirmed histologically. Although this abnormality is most often seen in the macula (posterior central retina), smaller cavities can be seen elsewhere in the retina, especially overlying blood vessels. When found over blood vessels these cavities do not seem to have as much diagnostic specificity. Although these lesions may heal with little visual sequelae, circular folds and scars within the retina may serve as a marker of previous shaking injury. Other sequelae of shaking include retinal detachment and atrophy of the optic nerve.

Sexually transmitted diseases

The exact diagnostic significance of sexually transmitted diseases affecting the eye in non-neonatal prepubertal children remains somewhat unclear. Two retrospective studies have identified cases in which gonorrhoeal conjunctivitis was transmitted non-sexually. Gonorrhoea cannot be transmitted to genital or oropharyngeal locations by any route other than sexual contact. Perhaps the mucosal lining of the eye represents a special site in this regard. In all the cases of non-sexual transmission there was a family member who had a genital infection and a completely negative evaluation for sexual abuse (including negative cultures for other sexually transmitted diseases at other sites, and an interview with the child by a person skilled and experienced in child sexual abuse).

Syphilis is the only organism that results in ocular effects exclusively through sexual contact. Although the presence of any other sexually transmitted disease should, at the very least, prompt consideration that possible covert sexual abuse has occurred, the possibility of non-sexual transmission to the eye of infections other than syphilis has not yet been disproved. With each of the infections, perhaps excepting ocular herpes and molloscum, a complete evaluation for sexual abuse is indicated. Reporting to child protective agencies should be reserved for those cases in which further evaluation confirms the suspicion of sexual abuse or fails to offer another plausible explanation.

Chronic and unusual visual symptoms or signs

Children may present with one of many functional ocular symptoms, including blinking, photophobia, eyelid pulling, eye rolling, and visual disturbances. Covert abuse is a rare cause of such symptoms but must always be considered when looking for stress factors that are commonly associated with functional illness. Likewise, chronic ocular signs or symptoms such as recurrent conjunctivitis or abnormalities in pupillary size should provoke consideration of Munchausen syndrome by proxy in the appropriate clinical setting (page 44). In addition to these two signs, only one other case of Munchausen syndrome by proxy with ocular findings (recurrent periorbital cellulitis) has been described.

Ocular manifestations of sexually transmitted diseases

Gonorrhoea*	Purulent conjunctivitis with possible spontaneous corneal perforation
Chlamydia†	Chronic conjunctivitis
Herpes simplex virus‡	Keratitis, conjunctivitis, intraocular inflammation, retinal necrosis
Human papilloma virus†	Conjunctival papillomas
HIV‡	Intraocular inflammation, retinal infections (for example, cytomegalovirus, toxoplasmosis), optic neuropathy, eye movement disorders
Syphilis	Intraocular inflammation, retinal vasculitis, optic neuropathy, eye movement disorders, and many other ocular abnormalities
Pubic lice†	Eyelash infestation
Molloscum*	Eyelid/periorbital lesions with possible secondary conjunctivitis

* Non-sexual transmission to eye in non-neonates documented.
† Route of transmission to eye not well studied.
‡ Non-sexual transmission to non-neonates documented.

Further reading

Greenwald MJ. The shaken baby syndrome. *Seminars Ophthalmol* 1990;5:202–15.

Levin AV. Ocular manifestations of child abuse. *Ophthalmol Clin N Am* 1990;3:249–64.

Levin AV. Ophthalmologic manifestations of child abuse. In: Ludwig S, Kornberg A, eds. *Child abuse: a medical reference.* 2nd ed. New York: Churchill Livingstone, 1992.

BURNS AND SCALDS

Chris Hobbs

<table>
<tr><td>

Accident:
lapse in usual protection given to the child

Neglect:
inadequate or negligent parenting, failing to protect the child

Abuse:
deliberately inflicted injury

</td></tr>
</table>

Accidental burns and scalds in children occur because of a lapse in the usual protection given to the child. Neglected children may be burnt because of inadequate or negligent parenting, which is a failure to protect the child, whereas in abused children burns and scalds are deliberately inflicted.

Burns and scalds within the range of child abuse are seen as serious injuries, as sadistic and linked with the sexual or violent arousal of an adult, and as punitive to evoke fear ("I'll teach him a lesson").

Prevalence

Deliberately inflicted burns and scalds are found in 10% of physically abused children, 5% of sexually abused children, and 1–16% of all children presenting at hospital with burns and scalds. This form of physical abuse is, however, under-recognised and under-reported because diagnosis may be difficult.

The peak age of children accidentally burning or scalding themselves is during the second year; the peak age of children being deliberately burnt is during the third year.

Left: Contact burns in 2 year old boy with developmental retardation who was abused by his mother. Burns to penis were also present.
Right: End of curtain wire heated in fire that was responsible for burns

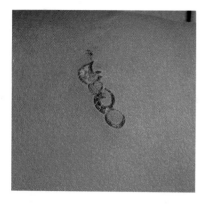
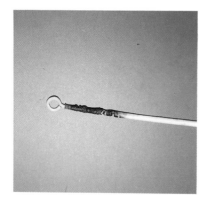

Cratered deep cigarette burn in typical site on back of hand in 5 year old boy, who also said, "Mummy put her fingers in my bottom"

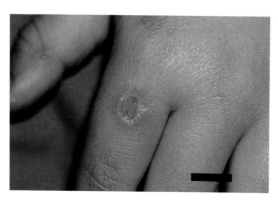

Types of thermal injury

Scalds—These are caused by hot water—for example, in drinks, liquid food, and baths. Scalds cause blisters and the affected skin peels in sheets and is soggy and blanched. They have a characteristic shape: they follow the contours of clothes and are enhanced by them, and drip, pour, and splash patterns are seen. The depth of injury is variable and contoured.

Contact, dry burns—Such burns are caused by hot objects, usually metallic, and electric fires. The injury looks like a brand mark, sharply demarcated and with the shape of the object that caused it. The burn is dry and tends to be of a uniform depth.

Burns from flames—These are caused by fires and matches and may be identified by charring and by singed hairs.

Cigarette burns—These leave a circular mark and a tail if the cigarette was brushed against the skin. In physical abuse the burn tends to form a crater and to scar because the injury is deep. The injury may be multiple but is not particularly common.

Electrical burns—These are small but deep with exit and entry points.

Friction burns—These occur when, for example, a child is dragged across a floor. Bony prominences are affected and the blisters are broken.

Chemical burns—These may cause staining and scarring of the skin.

Radiant burns—These are caused by radiant energy—for example, from a fire or the sun. Injury is usually extensive and affects one aspect of an arm or leg or the body and is limited by clothing. The skin shows erythema and blistering. Such burns occur in children who are made to stand in front of a fire.

Depth of burns and scalds

The depth of burns depends on the temperature and duration of exposure. In the case of hot water immersion for adults the following serve as approximate guides:

- 52·7°C (127°F)—1 minute for full thickness scald
- 54·4°C (130°F)—30 seconds
- 65·5°C (150°F)—2 seconds.

Above 60°C (140°F) children's skin burns in one quarter of the time of adult skin. The temperature of hot water in many homes as it leaves the tap is as high as 60°C (140°F), thus increasing the risks of injury to children.

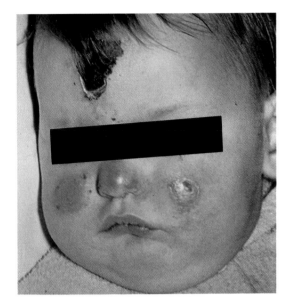

Friction burn in baby pulled across carpet by sibling

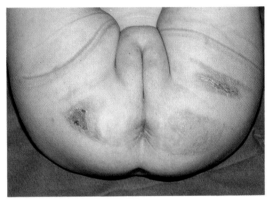

Examination of this 18 month old girl's older brother at school for an unexplained burn on his back led to chance discovery of these old, healing, partially infected contact burns for which parents had not sought treatment. The source was fire; both children had been abused

Relationship between temperature and duration of exposure and injury

Transfer of heat from hot water is more predictable than in other situations—for example contact burns from hot objects. Obviously maintenance of close contact, with air excluded, will be prevented by rapid reflex withdrawal of the part, which cannot occur in the same way with a scald. For this reason the mechanism by which contact was maintained must be ascertained in anything other than minor contact burns. Deep contact burns are likely to occur only when enforced contact has taken place.

Deep burns leave permanent scars which can provide later evidence of physical abuse.

History of physical abuse

In physical abuse the history of the burn is not consistent with the injury—for example, a 2 year old is said to have got into a bath of warm water, turned on the hot tap, and burnt both feet. There is a delay in seeking treatment or treatment is avoided altogether, the injury being discovered by chance.

The parent may deny that the injury is a burn when it clearly is and offer an unlikely explanation. The doctor may be told that the child did it to himself or that a sibling did. The incident is often unwitnessed ("I didn't see what happened, but he might have . . .") whereas in accidental injury to toddlers and young children parents are usually very clear what happened, even if they did not themselves see it.

A child who has been deliberately burnt may say that it did not hurt and the parent may tell the doctor that the child did not cry, which represents denial of what has happened. Alternatively, the child's history may disagree with that of the parents. The mother might say that the child fell over on to the fire and the child tell a nurse quietly, "Mummy did it."

In physical abuse repeated burns are seen. In accidents once is usually enough for most parents and children.

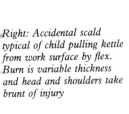

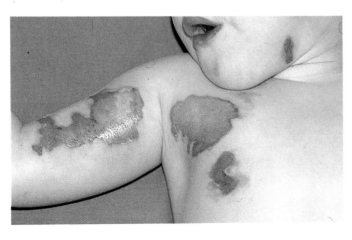

Left: Scalds from coffee thrown by drunken father at 3 year old girl producing scattered splash effect. Differentiation from accidental scalds from pouring liquids may be difficult

Right: Accidental scald typical of child pulling kettle from work surface by flex. Burn is variable thickness and head and shoulders take brunt of injury

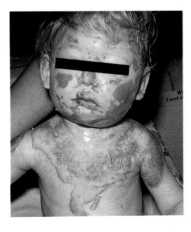

Burns and scalds

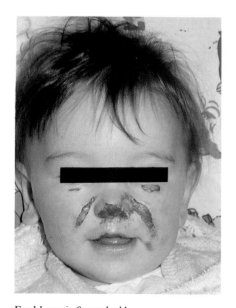

Food burns in 9 month old child with failure to thrive that allegedly occurred when he was left alone with bowl of hot food. Parents' refusal to allow admission to hospital, absence of burns in mouth, and failure to match burn with supplied utensil left serious doubts

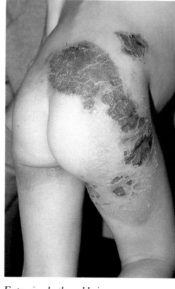

Extensive bath scalds in 3 year old girl failing to thrive. Central part of buttock spared where pressed on to cool base of bath—"hole in doughnut" effect. Abuse suspected but unproved

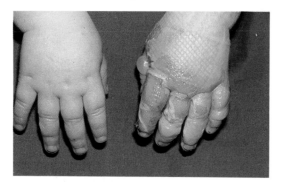

Admitted abuse in boy aged 3 years. Hand was held under hot tap

Important sites and patterns

Accidental burns

Most common scalds in toddlers and older infants occur when the child pulls kettles, pans, or cups of hot water or drinks from a kitchen unit or table. The scald affects the face, shoulders, upper arms, and upper trunk.

Accidental scalding from hot baths leaves an irregular mark with splashes.

Contact burns tend to be superficial, except in accidents with electric bar fires in which the hand sticks to the bar and sustains deep destructive burns to the palm.

Burns due to physical abuse

Non-accidental burns affect the face and head, perineum, buttocks and genitalia, the hands, and the feet and legs.

Cigarette burns may be seen on the face and head. Burns may be seen around rather than in the mouth when food has been pushed into the face.

To punish wetting and soiling misdemeanours or cure problems with wetting, abusing parents may dip the child's buttocks into a bath of hot water. The centre of the burn may show sparing where the buttocks pressed on the bath—the so-called "hole in the doughnut" effect. Burns to the perineum and genitalia may be part of sexual abuse.

Hands commonly show burns to the dorsal surface in physical abuse, whereas in accidents—for example, with an electric fire—the palm is affected. Hands are burnt by being held under a tap or on to hot objects.

The soles of the feet may show contact or cigarette burns. Burns on the feet and ankles may show a stocking or glove distribution with no splash marks and a clear tide mark when they have been caused by forced immersion in a sink or bath. Contact burns from fires (grid marks), irons, and curling tongs may also be seen on the legs and feet.

Characteristics of parents and children

Parents may be hostile, abusive to staff, and angry. They may refuse to allow the child to be admitted despite the need for treatment or threaten to discharge the child prematurely. Mothers who burn their children may be depressed, withdrawn, seeking help, and be themselves victims of child abuse (often sexual abuse).

In contrast to parents of accidentally burnt children abusing parents may show a lack of concern for the child or a lack of guilt. Parents of accidentally burnt children are often

Boy aged 30 months with symmetrical stocking scalds (full thickness in part) to both feet and superficial scald to buttock with unaffected intervening areas. History of unwitnessed bathing accident but forced immersion later admitted

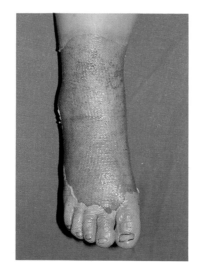

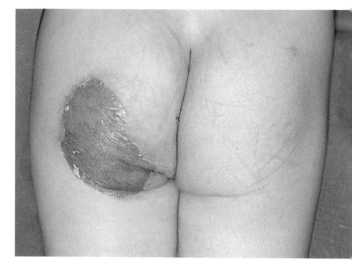

defensive, guilty, and dislike being questioned about the cause of the injury, which should not be misinterpreted as evidence of physical abuse.

A disturbed interaction between parent and child may show itself as anger and hostility towards the child—"It's his fault"—or as disregard of, or an inability to cope with, the child's behaviour. Abused children may be excessively withdrawn, passive, and uncomplaining about dressings or extremely anxious, hyperactive, angry, and rebellious, especially in the children's ward. In older children a reluctance to talk about their injury and how it occurred is worrying.

Assessment

Assessment is multidisciplinary and entails the participation of doctors (general practitioner, accident and emergency doctor, plastic surgeon, and consultant paediatrician), nurses, health visitors, social workers, police officers, and forensic scientists. In other words, the social services, the primary health care team, the hospital team, and the police need to liaise.

Visits to the child's home with the police may be required to inspect the bathroom, kitchen, fires, and household equipment.

History—This must be detailed and give the exact time of the incident, the sequence of events, and the action taken. Is the child's developmental ability consistent with what he is said to have done? For example, could an 18

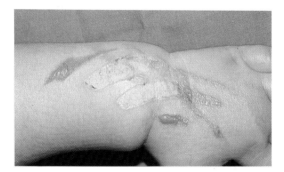

Inflicted contact burn on gas fire in 4 year old boy. Mother said dog knocked him on to fire when she was out of room. Child said that his brother did it. Burn was old and healing and was not presented for treatment. Child kept away from school

Partial thickness grid burn on back of wrist of 11 month old baby allegedly caused by older sibling. Mother later admitted responsibility for this single injury

month old child climb into a bath in the way stated?

Examination—Draw, measure, and photograph the injury. Manipulate the child's posture to discover his position when the injury occurred. Record the depth of the injury in relation to the temperature. Look for other injuries and look for signs of sexual abuse during genital and anal examinations. Assess the child's demeanour, behaviour, and development. In physical abuse failure to thrive and a delay in acquiring language are common. Finally, always ask the child what happened.

Differential diagnosis

When there is a lesion and no history of a burn skin infection or disease should be considered. Examples of conditions that may mimic burns are epidermolysis bullosa, impetigo, papular urticaria, contact dermatitis, and severe nappy rash.

Improbable accidents can occur. For example, a child could be burnt by vinegar, as concentrated vinegar (glacial acetic acid) has a pH of 1·6. In addition, the buckles of seat belts or black vinyl seats heated by the sun have caused injuries that have been confused with physical abuse. In general central heating radiators are safe but hands have been badly burnt when they have been trapped behind one, and the injudicious use of hot water bottles for babies has resulted in burns that are caused by neglect rather than abuse.

Anaesthesia, an inability to move, or neurological deficit caused by a congenital insensitivity to pain, syringomyelia, spina bifida, mental disability, cerebral palsy, and epilepsy may be associated with unusual burns and scalds.

Neglect should also be considered. Children left alone at home have an increased risk of dying in house fires. Fireguards are required by law for children under 12. Negligent parents may fail to seek treatment when their children are burnt. Therefore the effects of neglect are serious and should also be reported to protective agencies.

Further reading

Feldman KW. Child abuse by burning. In: Helfer RE, Kempe RS, eds. *The battered child.* 4th ed. Chicago: Chicago University Press, 1987:197.
Hight DW, Bakalar HR, Lloyd J. Inflicted burns in children. Recognition and treatment. *JAMA* 1979;**242**:517–20.
Hobbs CJ. When are burns not accidental? *Arch Dis Child* 1986;**61**:357–61.
Keen JH, Lendrum J, Wolman B. Inflicted burns and scalds in children. *Br Med J* 1975;**iv**:268–9.
Lenoski EF, Hunter KA. Specific patterns of inflicted burn injuries. *J Trauma* 1977;**17**:842.

POISONING

Roy Meadow

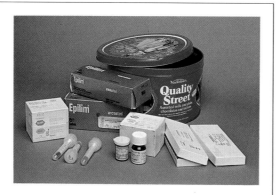

A 3 year old child presented with recurrent bouts of drowsiness. At first the mother denied giving drugs inappropriately but subsequently displayed them together with the container in which she kept them.

Accidental poisoning is very common; non-accidental poisoning is uncommon but more serious. Accidental poisoning commonly occurs in toddlers aged 2 to 4 who explore the world with their mouth and try out any medicines, tablets, or other liquids that they find. The parent finds the 3 year old with an empty bottle in the bathroom or kitchen and is unsure how much the child has ingested. Usually the child has swallowed little or nothing and it is a poisoning scare rather than a true poisoning event. Less than 15% of the thousands of children presenting to hospital because of accidental poisoning develop symptoms from the drug; death is extremely rare. Death from non-accidental poisoning is more common.

It is important to be aware that sometimes the parent will have poisoned the child. Therefore the story must always be checked to make sure that it makes sense—could that young a child have had access to those particular tablets? (2 year old children probably cannot reach the top shelf of the kitchen cupboard, neither can they easily unwrap individually foil packed tablets or open a child resistant container. Child resistant containers are not childproof, but they do delay the child's access to the contents.)

Detecting non-accidental poisoning

Deliberate poisoning mainly occurs in children below the age of $2\frac{1}{2}$ years. Children who have been poisoned by a parent are likely to present in four main ways.

(1) The child presents as a poisoning scare in which the parent rushes the child to hospital claiming that the child has ingested the drug accidentally.

(2) The child presents with inexplicable symptoms and signs, usually of acute onset. These are summarised in the box on p 25, together with some of the drugs that have been given intentionally by parents to children.

(3) The child presents with recurrent unexplained illnesses that have the features in the box—for example, recurrent episodes of drowsiness or hyperventilation. These sorts of patients overlap with those for whom parents create false illness (Munchausen syndrome by proxy) by other means.

(4) The child may be moribund or dead when first seen by the doctor.

In all cases check for other forms of abuse and for sudden unexplained deaths in other members of the family.

Motive

The motive for poisoning varies and includes parents who are vindictive and seeking to teach their child a lesson, parents who are themselves addicted to drugs such as methadone or cannabis and involve the child from an early age, and parents who seek to make a healthy child seem to have a chronic illness.

Establishing poisoning

Identifying poisoning can be very difficult, even when the doctor is alert to the possibility. Most hospitals have a limited biochemical screen confined to major common drugs for urine samples, but there is no fully comprehensive toxicology screen available. Therefore the doctor's job is, firstly, to think of possible drugs responsible for the child's symptoms, secondly, to try to identify from the general practitioner or hospital records any

One of the commonest poisons given by parents is table salt—sodium chloride. Usually a child will excrete excess salt speedily in the urine but if deprived of water will be unable to do so. Then hypernatraemia develops, causing initial thirst and irritation followed by drowsiness and seizures. Death occurs in extreme cases. The high serum sodium concentration will be associated with an extremely high sodium concentration in the urine.

Symptoms and signs	Drug
Seizures and apnoeic spells	Salt (sodium chloride) Phenothiazines Tricyclic antidepressants Hydrocarbons
Hyperventilation	Salicylates Acids
Drowsiness and stupor	Hypnotics Insulin Aspirin Paracetamol Tricyclic antidepressants Anticonvulsants Phenothiazines Methadone Cannabis
Hallucinations	Atropine-like agents
Bizarre motor movements (myoclonic jerks, tremors, extrapyramidal signs)	Phenothiazines Metoclopramide Antihistamines
Vomiting	Emetics and many other drugs
Diarrhoea (with or without failure to thrive)	Laxatives, including magnesium hydroxide (Milk of Magnesia) and phenolphthalein Salt
Haematemesis	Salicylates Iron
Ulcerated mouth	Corrosives
Thirst	Salt (with or without water deprivation)
Bizarre biochemical blood profile	Salt Insulin Salicylates Sodium bicarbonate

Sometimes the methods are so bizarre that they defy the commonsense reasoning of a normal person. You have to accept that parents do incredible things and that a determined parent can find ways of poisoning a child, even when under the closest supervison. Mothers have injected insulin into intravenous lines, poured medicine into a gastrostomy tube, put nasogastric tubes down into the child's stomach to administer particularly noxious solutions that the child would otherwise not take, secreted tablets in their mouth that they have passed on to the child with a kiss, and secreted drugs behind the glass eyeball of the teddy bear they have given to the child. The essential first step is to identify the poison and only then to start puzzling about how the child was given it.

If poisoning is suspected every chance should be given to the parent to explain how the child came to be given the poison. Many parents give drugs, tonics, and folk remedies to their child without telling doctors. Some are fearful of discussing it because they think the doctor would disapprove; others are embarrassed by trying a rather naive remedy for their child. Therefore the doctor should sympathetically explore with the parent the ways in which a child might have ingested a particular poison. This is particularly important for people from unconventional backgrounds or from different ethnic cultures, who may use many different souces of health advice apart from the NHS.

Poison centres

Poison centres provide advice about the constituents of many proprietary and household products and also about treatment. They may also be helpful when you are faced with a child who has possibly been poisoned by suggesting ways of identifying the drug.

Poison information services

Belfast, 0232 240503
Birmingham, 021 554 3801
Cardiff, 0222 709901
Dublin, 0001 379964
Edinburgh, 031 229 2477
Leeds, 0532 430175
London, 071 635 9191
Newcastle 091 232 5131

There are six regional forensic laboratories in England and Wales, each serving six or more police forces, and the London Metropolitan Police has its own laboratory. In general their work comes directly from the police, though some will accept work from doctors through the local Home Office pathologist (whose name and address can be obtained from the local coroner's office)

drugs that might be present in that household or to which the mother has access, and then, thirdly, to ask the laboratory to look specifically for that drug in the child's urine or blood. It is worth finding out if the parent's jobs give them access to particular drugs—for example, if a parent is a nurse or works in a hospital. Until such information is available samples of blood, urine, and vomit, if available, should be kept safely in the refrigerator. A few drugs are radio-opaque so a straight abdominal radiograph may be helpful if taken within a few hours of ingestion.

It is particularly important to preserve samples of blood, urine, and tissues when a child is brought in moribund with apparent encephalopathy, liver failure, bleeding disorder, or bizarre biochemical results. When such children die it is mandatory to inform the coroner. Whenever there is a strong suspicion of poisoning the police should be informed; their regional forensic laboratories can be extremely helpful in analysing samples for they have one of the more detailed screening systems, but even these regional laboratories cannot screen for everything and they do their job best if they are given some idea of the type of drug to look for.

It is more important in the first place to try to identify the drug than the method by which the parent has given the drug to the child.

Further reading
Rogers D, Tripp J, Bentovim A, Robinson A, Berry D, Goulding R. Non-accidental poisoning: an extended syndrome of child abuse. *BMJ* 1976;i:793–6.
Meadow R. Non-accidental salt poisoning. *Arch Dis Child* 1993; **68**: 448–52.

SUFFOCATION

Roy Meadow

> The tyrannous and bloody act is done;
> The most arch deed of piteous massacre
> That ever yet this land was guilty of . . .
> . . . we smothered the most replenished sweet
> work of nature . . .
>
> Sir James Tyrrell after the murder of the two
> child princes in the tower.
> SHAKESPEARE, *Richard III*

Asphyxia is an uncommon but serious form of child abuse. The commonest form is smothering and the abuser is usually the child's mother, who uses her hand, a pad of rolled up clothing, or a pillow to cause mechanical obstruction to the child's airways. Less commonly she presses the child's face against her chest, encloses the child's head in a plastic bag, or strangles by pressure on the child's neck.

Clinical features

Smothering happens to young children under the age of 3 years, most being infants under the age of 1 year. They may present to doctors either as sudden unexplained deaths ("cot deaths"), moribund ("near miss cot deaths"), or repetitively as cyanotic or floppy children whom the mother alleges to have had an episode at home—which is presumed by doctors to have been an apnoeic attack or a seizure. (If a mother describes a young baby having stopped breathing or having seemed unconscious for a short time a doctor will probably consider that the baby has had an apnoeic attack, whereas in an older child he or she is more likely to consider the same description to have been a seizure.)

A small proportion of babies currently certified as having died from "the sudden infant death syndrome" have been killed by their parent. It is important to recognise this but not to overemphasise it—for over 90% of parents who suffer the sudden death of their infant are blameless. The proportion of sudden infant deaths caused by a parent is uncertain and will vary from year to year and from country to country. The sort of psychosocial investigation required to identify such deaths is difficult to pursue and has been completed in only a few studies. Emery concludes, from his own and the work of others, that the proportion is less than one in 10 but more than one in 50. Smothering by the mother seems to be the usual mechanism. Some of the infants have had previous recurrent episodes apnoea or seizures that may have been investigated thoroughly in a conventional radiological, biochemical, or electrophysiological way without proper consideration being given to child abuse as a possible cause. Warning features that the sudden infant death syndrome may have been caused by a mother smothering her child are:

- Previous episodes of unexplained apnoea, seizures, or "near miss cot death"
- An infant aged over 6 months
- Previous unexplained disorders affecting that child
- Other unexplained deaths of children in the same family.

For some children the smothering is associated with other forms of child abuse, particularly physical abuse and Munchausen syndrome by proxy.

Some mothers smother their child when they are feeling violent hatred towards their baby, others do it in a repetitive systematic way, taking their child regularly to the doctor each time that they have smothered their child for long enough to make him or her unconscious. For others it is an impulsive action at a time of frustration or stress at home.

And Then There Were None

During their 14 years as parents, Mary Beth and Joseph Tinning buried nine children. Until the last death, authorities never suspected wrongdoing. How could this happen?

THE GUARDIAN
Friday December 2 1988

First child 'smothered,' said mother

A MOTHER accused of murdering her second child...

Upstate Mother Is Held

Continued From Page 1

2-year-old had been hospitalized for what was called a fall down a flight of stairs. Social service...

After 9 Babies Die in 14 Years, Mother Is Held

By AMY WALLACE
Special to The New York Times

...TADY, N.Y., Feb...

It was not until Wednesday, when the police charged Mrs. Tinning, who is 43 years old, with suffocating her daughter...

said there might have been incomplete examinations of the deaths and lapses communication among doc...

Signs of smothering

Smothering is violent; a young child who cannot breathe struggles and tries to get air. The smothering needs considerable force, even when a child is young: the child has to be laid down on his back or against something firm for the mother to press hard on his face, alternatively the child is clutched closely into her chest. Despite the obvious violence entailed the signs may be very few. In general, someone who is asphyxiated tends to develop multiple petechiae on the face, particularly on the eyelids, as a result of the raised blood pressure, lack of oxygen, and retention of carbon dioxide. There may be congestive changes in the face too. Hand pressure on the face may leave thumbmarks or fingerprints around the nose or mouth or abrasions inside the mouth with bruising of the gums; but more often smothering is done with a pillow or with clothing and no external pressure marks are visible, and quite often neither petechiae nor swelling of the face are apparent. All forms of asphyxiation may be associated with some bleeding from the nose or mouth, but it is not inevitable. Thus a smothered infant may show no signs at all to the most experienced clinician or forensic pathologist. Although generally the smothering has to persist for a minute to cause seizures—longer to cause brain damage and perhaps two minutes (depending upon other circumstances) to cause death—damage may be more sudden and catastrophic if the child, as a result of the sudden assault, has a cardiac arrest or vomits and chokes. Severe smothering may lead to the appearance of pulmonary oedema on the chest radiograph.

Differential diagnosis

Unexplained episodes of apnoea or a seizure are commonly reported by mothers of young babies. Sometimes an anxious mother perceives illness that is not there or overinterprets the periodic breathing and normal movements of a healthy baby. Therefore in all such cases it is worth trying to get a description of the episodes from another relative. This is particularly important if the mother is suspected of causing the episodes.

True apnoea, in which the breathing stops for 20 seconds or more and is followed by bradycardia, cyanosis, or pallor, is frightening and often unexplained. It is more likely in small preterm babies and usually starts in the neonatal period. In early life both respiratory syncytial virus infection and whooping cough can be associated with spells of apnoea in previously well infants; the apnoea may precede the cough or other respiratory signs by a few days.

Whenever apnoea starts unexpectedly in a previously well baby it must be investigated thoroughly. The investigations should include careful checks for cardiac or respiratory disorder, oesophageal reflux, and a biochemical or seizure disorder. When these investigations give normal results consideration should be given to whether the episodes are being caused by the mother; if the episodes are frequent a period in hospital without the mother might be the wisest course. If the episodes are frequent when at home and absent when in hospital away from the mother, the mother is probably responsible—by acts of either omission or commission. Some hospital units are able to arrange covert video recording of the infant and mother in hospital. As a diagnostic test video surveillance is highly specific since filmed evidence of suffocation provides conclusive proof. But it is not very sensitive as most abuse occurs at home and even if the mother does suffocate her child in hospital she may well not do so during the period of video surveillance.

Sudden infant death syndrome (cot death)

The sudden infant death syndrome is the commonest category of death in Britain for infants aged between 1 month and 1 year. The label is given when no cause is found for the death of a previously well infant. Roughly two per 1000 live births are affected. It is commonest in the first five months of life and happens to previously well children who have not had episodes of apnoea or other unexplained illness. Recurrence within a family is extemely rare. The parents are not responsible or to blame for the tragic death of their child.

Further reading
Meadow R. Suffocation, recurrent apnoea and sudden infant death. *J Pediatrics* 1990;**117**:351–7.
Newlands M, Emery JS. Child abuse and cot deaths. *Child Abuse Negl* 1991;**15**:275–8.
Rosen CL, Frost Jr JD, Bricker T, Tarnow JK, Gillette PC, Dunlavy S. Two siblings with recurrent cardiorespiratory arrest: Munchausen syndrome by proxy or child abuse? *Pediatrics* 1983;**71**:7154–20.
Samuels MP, McClaughlin W, Jacobson RR, Poets CF, Southall DP. Fourteen cases of imposed upper airway obstruction. *Arch Dis Child* 1992;**67**:162–70.

EMOTIONAL ABUSE AND NEGLECT

David Skuse

Emotional abuse and neglect of children may take many forms, from a lack of care for their physical needs, through a failure to provide consistent love and nurture, to overt hostility and rejection. Deleterious effects upon developing children are correspondingly diverse and tend to vary with age. In infancy neglect of physical care is likely to produce the most obvious consequences and developmental delays are also found. Preschool children may additionally present with disorders of social and emotional adjustment. Older children are likely to show behavioural problems at school, which are often accompanied by extensive learning difficulties. Emotional abuse is rarely the sole reason for seeking child protection through legal action, yet evidence is accumulating that its long term consequences upon social, emotional, and cognitive development may be far reaching and profound. There is growing awareness that not only do many, if not most, cases of physical abuse and neglect occur in a context of emotional maltreatment, but it is the psychological aspects of the maltreatment that are of the greatest significance for future adjustment.

Defining features

Emotional abuse refers to the habitual verbal harassment of a child by disparagement, criticism, threat and ridicule, and the inversion of love; by verbal and non-verbal means rejection and withdrawal are substituted. Neglect comprises both a lack of physical caretaking and supervision and a failure to engage the developmental needs of the child in terms of cognitive stimulation. Although direct observation of parenting may raise suspicions about the presence of emotional abuse and neglect, the diagnosis is usually suggested by its consequences in the child: "the severe adverse effect on the behaviour and emotional development of a child caused by persistent or severe emotional ill-treatment or rejection."[1] All abuse entails some emotional ill treatment. There is often accompanying physical or sexual abuse. Without signs of physical or sexual maltreatment and disclosure of specific abusive activities, however, it is still possible to recognise characteristic groups of features that demand further investigation. Current knowledge on the subject does not yet allow us causally to link specific patterns of maltreatment to particular delays and disorders. In addition, the symptoms and signs to be described are not invariably indicative of abuse and neglect. But the cessation of abuse and its substitution with sensitive care—often in an alternative home— is usually followed by a rapid and dramatic improvement in developmental attainments, behaviour, and socioemotional adjustment.

Infants

Neglect of the physical and emotional nurture of an infant is likely to result in various signs and symptoms that should be fairly easily recognised. The aspects of physical development that are affected are those that demand the closest attention from caregivers. Babies are dependent creatures: they need to be fed regularly, to be kept in a reasonably dry and warm environment, and to have their bowel and bladder functions taken care of. If they are habitually cold and wet they will contract recurrent infections; if they do not have their nappies changed regularly they will develop nappy rash, which if neglected may cause scarring; if they are not fed adequately they will fail to thrive. Failure to thrive is usually defined as an exceptionally poor rate of growth in which weight (and often length) becomes increasingly divergent from normal age standardised values in the population. There are many reasons why such a pattern of growth may occur. Recent population surveys show that it is only exceptionally associated with abuse or deliberate neglect—even in non-organic cases. In families in which abuse is suspected other evidence to support those suspicions should be sought.

When there has been serious neglect social and psychomotor skills are also likely to be affected. If there has been no encouragement to acqure skills such as sitting, crawling, and

---

Key features in infants

Physical	Failure to thrive
	Recurrent and persistent minor infections
	Frequent attendances at casualty departments or admissions to hospital
	Unexplained bruising
	Severe nappy rash
Development	General delay
Behaviour	Attachment disorders: anxious, avoidant
	Lack of social responsiveness

walking the infant may show developmental delay. Infants are innately sociable: they enjoy interacting with others, adults or children. A severely neglected infant will not have learnt the joy of reciprocal smiling and laughter and so may not try to elicit attention. Although the concept of infant depression is controversial, increasing evidence suggests that the infants of some depressed (and therefore comparatively neglectful) mothers do show characteristic social responses, such as withdrawal, "looking away" behaviour and emotional flattening. Severely understimulated infants may use self stimulatory behaviours such as persistently banging their head or rocking.

Selective attachments to important adults in an infant's life begin to be established around 6 to 8 months of age. A neglected or abused infant may show an unusual pattern of attachment. Usually the experience of consistent and sensitive parenting leads a child to feel safe and secure with the primary caregiver, even in the presence of a stranger. In an unfamiliar setting such as a surgery or clinic the wish to explore will be counterbalanced by a wish to stay close to the parent. Infants who have been abused or neglected lack this sense of security. They do not have sufficient confidence to explore their surroundings and seem ill at ease, whining and unhappy, and cling to their caregiver, who responds with irritation. Alternatively, there may be little evidence for any attachment behaviour and the infant either roams around the room in a completely non-directed fashion (attributable perhaps to high anxiety) or creeps quietly into a corner and observes the proceedings warily (frozen watchfulness). Recent research has shown, however, that large differences in the availability of, and nurture by, a caregiver do not always correlate with variations in attachment.

Preschool children

The physical consequences of persistent abuse and neglect through the preschool period often include poor growth, not only in height and weight but also in the circumference of the head. Dramatic increases in head size have been documented when abused children have been removed to a nurturing alternative environment. Associated indicators of abuse include recurrent minor

unexplained injuries, especially bruising. It is important to be aware of the distribution of bruises that is likely to indicate squeezing, choking, and slapping.

The development of communication between children, even those who cannot talk, and their caregivers is a subtle process with its own set of shared expectations and rules of operation. Persistent neglect and abuse will prevent the establishment of a "mutual faith in a shared world". Retardation in the development of receptive and expressive language will result, possibly exacerbated by recurrent inadequately treated middle ear infections and partial deafness. When the emotional abuse has been severe a child may become virtually mute. Language development seems to be especially vulnerable to the effects of a severely depriving environment.

The main indicators of emotional abuse and neglect of preschool children are usually behavioural. As long as the child does not mix in a social setting no problems may be reported. In a nursery school or day nursery, however, the child may show many and characteristic disorders. Attention span is commonly extremely limited: the child cannot settle to any task for more than a few seconds. This probably reflects a lack of attempts to engage the child's attention at home, but it may also indicate profound anxiety. Poor attention is often associated with excessive activity: such children may be described as hyperactive, although there is no evidence that most overactive preschool children have been abused. Aggressive disorders of conduct are an additional problem, and children who are observed persistently to hit or swear at their caregivers in the consulting room must be regarded as being at risk.

Peer relationships will inevitably be problematic as persistently abused children do not develop sufficient social maturity to play cooperatively. Therefore their relationships with other children may be characterised by a combination of aggression and withdrawal. Social relations will also be impaired by a lack of selective attachments; thus abused toddlers may show indiscriminately friendly behaviour that is qualitatively different from normal temperamental diversity and unlike behaviours reflective of broad social experience. Such children elicit intimate physical contact from complete strangers—they may end up on your lap within a few minutes of meeting—and seem to crave physical contact ("touch hunger"), even in the presence of their primary caregiver.

School children

In the child who has reached school age the effects of long term abuse and neglect occasionally lead to a characteristic syndrome of short stature coupled with certain behavioural and emotional problems. In many cases, however, there is no evidence of an effect on growth and the main indicators of abuse are to be found in poor social and

---

Key features in preschool children

Physical	Short stature
	Microcephaly
	Unkempt and dirty
Development	Language delayed
	Attention span limited
	Socioemotional immaturity
Behaviour	Overactive
	Aggressive and impulsive
	Indiscriminate friendliness
	Seeks physical contact from strangers

emotional adjustment, behaviour problems, and learning difficulties.

School may be unable to compensate for the long term lack of cognitive stimulation at home because abused children have tremendous problems attending to learning tasks. The failure in concentration is often coupled with physical overactivity of such a degree that the child is regarded as disruptive and may be referred for assessment for special education.

Persistent denigration and rejection will inevitably cause a lowering of self esteem; children who feel they are worthless may carry a huge burden of guilt for their behaviour. They may seem depressed and persistently apologise for trivial and meaningless supposed misdemeanours. For example, an abused 5 year old seen recently at her first visit to a child guidance clinic apologised to the therapist for not having saved him a piece of her birthday cake; her birthday had been three months previously. Such a poor self image is not really compatible with forming and keeping friendships at school; the social skills needed to negotiate such relationships have never been learnt. Thus the emotionally abused child stands alone at playtime or is seen drifting around the periphery of small groups engaged in their own pursuits. Sometimes more able children develop a coping strategy whereby their main social interaction is with adults—that is, with teachers rather than pupils. They show a pseudomaturity that belies their lack of sense of self worth and their longing for affection and stability. When the abuse has been coupled with a style of interaction that is aggressive and threatening the child may show similar behaviour to pupils and teachers. Such behaviour may also be habitual because at home it is the only way of attracting attention.

In extreme cases of emotional abuse and neglect patterns of behaviour are so unusual or bizarre that they inevitably draw attention to the child. Self mutilation, from skin picking to deliberate self injury with knives or glass, is one. Others include repetitive rocking or other self stimulatory activities, including sexual behaviours. Unusual patterns of defecation or urination are worrying in school children. Children who urinate or defecate in their clothes in class may be shunned as being smelly by their peers; perhaps that is how they view themselves—as disgusting and unpleasant individuals. Pools of urine or piles of faeces in the corridor or playground are signs that the culprit is urgently in need of assessment for possible abuse.

Adolescence

Adolescent abuse is less well recognised than it should be; recent research suggests that up to half of all abusive incidents involve this age group but they are far less likely to be reported to protective services than their equivalent among younger children. All forms of maltreatment do occur, but sexual and psychological abuse predominate. Girls are more likely to be victims as they pass through adolescence than during earlier childhood, whereas boys are at greater risk at a younger age. A substantial number of abusive incidents have their onset at this time; they are not simply the continuation of an earlier established pattern of behaviour. In contrast to the picture of abuse and neglect in early childhood all socioeconomic groups are equally at risk, but families with step-parents are especially vulnerable. The detrimental consequences of psychological, sexual, and physical maltreatment on adolescent adjustment may be severe. An association has been found with contemporaneous and later suicide attempts, drug and alcohol misuse, running away, promiscuity, and delinquency.

Investigation and management

Children who are being emotionally abused or neglected may not be in immediate physical or moral danger, but their need for protection is not, for all that, diminished. It must be acknowledged, however, that there is limited scope in such cases for medical investigation in the absence of associated physical or sexual maltreatment. Doctors who suspect that a child is being emotionally abused should first seek the advice of a colleague who is experienced in such matters. If no local paediatrician or child psychiatrist is available an inquiry to a tertiary referral centre elsewhere in the country will often be met with a courteous and helpful response. Subsequently, it will be necessary to share concerns with the statutory services responsible for child protection.

[1] Department of Health and Social Security and the Welsh Office. *Working together under the Children Act 1989. A guide to arrangements for inter-agency cooperation for the protection of children from abuse.* London: HMSO, 1991.

Further reading

Downey G, Coyne, JC. Children of depressed parents: an integrative review. *Psychol Bull*, 1990;**180**:50–76.
Garbarino J. Troubled youth, troubled families: the dynamics of adolescent maltreatment. In: Cicchetti D, Carlson V, eds. *Child maltreatment*. New York: Cambridge University Press, 1989:685–706.
Skuse D. Epidemiological and definitional issues in failure to thrive. In: Woolston J, ed. *Child and adolescent psychiatric clinics of North America*. Philadelphia: WB Saunders, 1993; 2(1): 37–59.
Skuse D, Bentovim A. Physical and emotional maltreatment. In: Rutter M, Hersov L, eds. *Child and adolescent psychiatry. Modern approaches.* 3rd ed. Oxford: Blackwell Scientific (in press).

Key features in school children	
Physical	Short stature
	Poor hygiene
	Unkempt appearance
Development	Learning difficulties
	Lack of self esteem
	Poor coping skills
	Socioemotional immaturity
Behaviour	Disordered or few relationships
	Self stimulating or self injurious behaviour, or both
	Unusual patterns of defecation or urination, or both

ABUSE AND SHORT STATURE

David Skuse

Better is a dinner of herbs where love is than a
stalled ox and hatred therewith
Proverbs XV, 17

Many exceptionally short children with no
detectable organic disorder to account for their
condition have failed to grow because they
have been subjected to longstanding abuse and
neglect within their families. Such children
have characteristic patterns of behaviour that
should draw attention to their predicament.
The underlying aetiology of their short stature
is probably always dysfunctional endocrine
control of linear growth, but conventional
investigations, such as tests of the integrity of
the hypothalamic-pituitary axis, may give
misleading (false negative) results. The key to
the diagnosis is a good history. Failure to
recognise the condition may imperil not only
the children's future physical development but
also their intelligence, their social adjustment,
and their emotional wellbeing. Appreciable
numbers of children attending specialist
growth clinics suffer from this underdiagnosed
disorder, for which no really satisfactory
diagnostic label exists but which will be
referred to as psychosocial short stature.

Defining features

Psychosocial short stature is not recognised
as a distinct entity within the International
Classification of Diseases, a deficiency which
hampers clinical recognition, inhibits
epidemiological investigations into prevalence,
and limits research into its aetiology and
management. Nevertheless, four key features
can be determined which together provide
compelling evidence for a diagnostic category:
firstly, a characteristic clinical picture
comprising symptoms, signs, and the results of
physiological tests; secondly, a common
aetiology; thirdly, a well recognised natural
history without intervention; and fourthly, a
predictable favourable response to appropriate
management.

Clinical picture

Impaired linear growth may follow failure to
thrive in infancy; recent prospective
longitudinal studies have shown that many
affected children remain significantly shorter
than their peers at least until puberty. Failure
to thrive is not usually due to overt abuse or
neglect. The main reason is virtually always
chronic undernutrition. Children whose linear

growth is significantly retarded for that reason,
in the first year or two of life, do not usually
show much catch up growth subsequently,
even if their nutritional environment improves.
They are moderately short, usually 90–95% of
expected height for age. They show none of
the distinctive behavioural characteristics of
psychosocial short stature, although,
depending on the pattern of growth in the
period up to six months post-term, they may
suffer from mild to moderately impaired
cognitive and psychomotor abilities.

In contrast, children with psychosocial short
stature are not only exceptionally small for
their age, they have a range of distinctive
behavioural symptoms. The confusion with
failure to thrive arises because many, if not
most of them, did fail to thrive as infants. But
only a very small minority of such infants go
on to develop this condition. The diagnosis is
based on a distinctive combination of current
and historical features. It is not normally made
before 2 to 3 years, probably because the
neuropsychological and neurophysiological
mechanisms mediating the characteristic
features require a certain level of central
nervous system maturation to become evident.
Symptoms include: a disorder of biological
rhythms, predominantly of sleep and appetite;
a disorder of self regulation, especially of
defecation, urination, and attention; a disorder
of mood, predominantly depression, a poor
self image, and low self esteem; and finally,
disordered social relationships, including those
with peers and adults, both within and outside
the family of origin. The key aetiological factor
is emotional rejection, which is often found in
combination with unusual and sadistic forms
of physical and sexual abuse. Most abused
children do not display the characteristics of
psychosocial short stature, and commonly just
one child in a family is affected.

Our clinical experience suggests that twins,
both monozygotic and dizygotic, are at
increased risk. Not only is it usual for both
twins to be affected (we have never seen just
one of a pair with the condition), but the
proportion of affected children who are twins
is rather higher than would be expected by
chance.

Anthropometry

Typically, the child's height for age is far
below the third centile, between 85% and 90%
of expected height for age. Growth is often at

a low normal rate parallel to the centile line, although occasionally the condition presents with a variable and inconsistent trajectory. Weight for height is appropriate and head circumference is often in proportion. Skinfold thickness and mid-upper arm circumference are usually low normal. Body proportions are immature with comparatively short legs. Siblings and parents are typically of average stature.

Disorders of biological rhythms

Perhaps the most characteristic feature of this condition is hyperphagia. Although it used to be thought these children were short because they had been starved by their parents, this was a misinterpretation of the evidence. Some children who are short because they have failed to thrive long term are undernourished, but you are more likely to encounter a history of food fads and a reluctance to eat in those cases. Children whose growth problem is due to emotional abuse typically possess an insatiable appetite, often associated with polydipsia. A long history of disordered behaviour with food is recounted, of which wandering around the home at night in search of it is typical. Parents respond by taking preventive action, placing locks on the bedroom, kitchen, and cupboard doors. Large quantities of food are hoarded, usually in the child's room, in a way one consultant remarked was "like squirrels putting away nuts for the winter." Pica and the consumption of discarded food found in streets or wastebins can lead to gastrointestinal disturbance for which specialist opinion may

be sought. Because of the child's propensity to "steal" food he or she may be fed separately from other family members. Teachers can often provide vivid accounts of disordered and bizarre behaviour at school dinner times. It is typical for parents to claim that if they let their children eat as much as they wanted they would gorge until they vomited and even, in a few cases, would not desist even at that point, but would continue and consume their own vomit.

Sleep is disrupted by nocturnal wanderings and, often, by nightmares. There are some reports of an increase in active rapid eye movement (REM) sleep and a decrease in stages III and IV non-REM sleep relative to norms for the age group. Growth hormone release may be disrupted, although it is not entirely clear whether this relates to the sleep pattern. Provocation tests often show a low normal response which is difficult to interpret. A nocturnal profile of the pattern of growth hormone secretion often shows a diminished pulse amplitude, which has the unique characteristic of recovery within a very brief period in hospital.

Disorders of self regulation

Soiling may be an indicator of coincident sexual abuse. The usual story is not one of typical encopresis but comprises the following features. Firstly, there is a persistency and frequency that ensures it is usually a daily occurrence. Secondly, there are unusual patterns of associated behaviour—formed stools are concealed around the house and may even be found at school. Soiled clothing may also be disposed of in strange and devious ways, such as under carpets. Thirdly, faecal smearing is often reported, which, if it occurs principally in the child's bedroom, may indicate confinement for protracted periods.

Unusual patterns of urination are typical and may mislead the unwary by presenting as enuresis. Close questioning reveals the urination is as much over the bed as it is in it. The behaviour also occurs elsewhere in the house, behind cupboards, in fireplaces, in toy chests, and so on. There may be an exhibitionistic quality to the behaviour. It seems to be used primarily as an aggressive act. When sibling rivalry is a major component of family dysfunction urination occurs over the sibling's possessions.

Children with psychosocial short stature have poor attention and may present with "hyperactivity." Invariably, there are associated learning difficulties. Poor receptive and expressive language skills are usual, in combination with relatively less impaired non-verbal abilities. Affected children may be receiving special education on the grounds of mild to moderate mental retardation. Accordingly, it is essential to be aware that they have the potential for rapid and dramatic catch up cognitive growth on removal from their abusive environment.

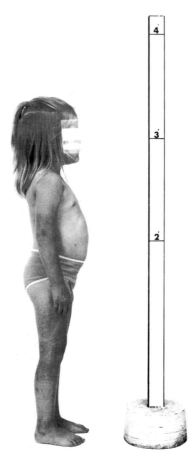

Girl aged 8 years 2½ months measuring 3' 4" (102 cm), a height age of 4 years

Disorders of mood

Parents often complain their child had a difficult temperament from the earliest days, would not settle into routines, was irritable, and disliked close physical contact. Relationships with parents and siblings are typically marked by sullen withdrawal or defiant hostility. At home and at school an unhappy mood predominates and self esteem is poor. Antisocial behaviours may be habitual, especially petty pilfering at school. The objects taken are often virtually worthless (pens, rubbers, trinkets), and the behaviour seems to be a response to an emotional need. In younger children apparently senseless destructive acts (smashing new toys) are indicative of inner turmoil and distress.

Parental efforts at controlling undesirable behaviours are met with defiance; there is a seeming tolerance to most physical punishments and, indeed, to physical pain and discomfort in general. Some parents resort to bizarre punitive methods, often with sadistic overtones—for example, shutting fingers in drawers, beating the soles of the feet, and making the child stand for prolonged periods with hands on head. Withdrawing food is a favourite technique for obvious reasons, and probably serves to exacerbate the food related behaviour disorders.

Disorders of social relationships

No children with so poor a self image as these unhappy subjects could enjoy the reciprocity and mutual regard that typifies a true friendship. They wander around on the fringes of their peer group, drifting into casual liaisons with those who are similarly alienated and consequently they are at high risk of becoming embroiled in antisocial activities. Relationships with adults are typified by sullen hostility and suspiciousness or, in some cases, by a promiscuous overfamiliarity which may have sexual undertones.

The depth of the alienation in family relationships may not be gauged by a casual observer in the surgery or outpatient clinic. Abused children may nevertheless be brought for medical attention and investigations. A hint of the degree to which they are regarded with contempt by their caretakers may be gathered from remarks made in your presence—for example, a father telling his 8 year old son "You've got custard for brains." Children with this condition often have an anxious attachment to their abusive parents and so will be very reluctant to separate from them. They may even be warned in your presence not to tell "porky pies." Faced with a profound fear of retribution on revealing the truth of their predicament, many children with psychosocial short stature will simply prefer to remain mute.

Management

When a diagnosis of emotional abuse leading to a delay in growth is suspected a coordinated response with the local social services department is necessary. A case conference will be held and the services of other experts such as a child psychiatrist and paediatric endocrinologist may be deemed necessary. Protection from further abuse should be the first priority and this will usually mean removing the child from the abusive environment. Sometimes it is possible to persuade the parents to give up the child voluntarily. In most cases legal proceedings must be instituted and there are three main sources of evidence which will serve as the basis for a successful intervention. Firstly, there is the evidence of the associated abuse. While emotional abuse as such is notoriously difficult to prove, a history of sexual abuse or physical abuse, or both, may be obtained together with associated physical signs. Secondly, there may be documented evidence that the affected child has shown catch up linear growth during a prolonged period in hospital or a former period of foster care. Thirdly, there may be evidence of a deterioration over time in cognitive abilities. Motor development will in general be less affected than skills based on language such as practical reasoning. Serial testing every six months or so with a standardised instrument such as the Griffiths scales can yield valuable information. Scores should be calculated as a

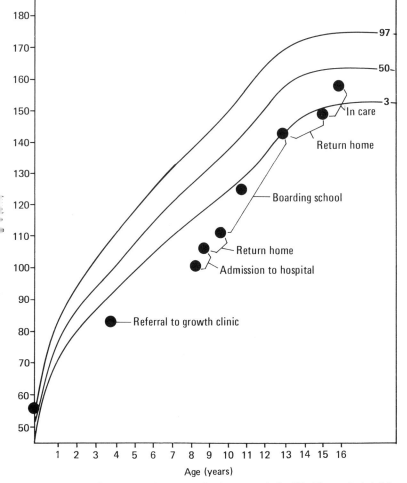

Growth curve of girl in figure on previous page related to events in her life. Her mother's height was 158 cm (25th centile) and her father's 178 cm (50th centile)

Key features

- Age range toddlers to adolescents
- Proportionate stunting
- Feeding behaviour grossly disturbed
- Unusual patterns of urination and defecation
- Mental development delayed
- Poor social adjustment
- Unhappy, irritable, defiant
- Antisocial behaviour
- Parents' attitude critical or belittling, or both
- Associated abuse especially sexual abuse
- Accelerated growth away from family
- Rapidly reversible growth hormone deficiency.

percentage, with the quotient of mental age divided by chronological age used to view trends.

Natural history

Absolutely characteristic of the syndrome is a dramatic increase in the children's velocity of linear growth once they have been removed from their abusive environment. It is not unusual to find a sixfold to tenfold increase within a few months. Mental development will also accelerate provided an appropriate attachment is established between the child and the carer, and the child is encouraged to learn in a comparatively structured and stimulating environment. If bizarre patterns of behaviour persist for longer than a few months, once the child is settled into a stable new home the question must be addressed, is the child now being abused by his or her new carers?

Should the child be returned home a diminution in growth rate will ensue. Unwary doctors may erroneously conclude that the potential for growth has now been fulfilled, especially if the subsequent trajectory is parallel to the centile lines.

Consider the growth curve on page 33, which is the growth record of the girl shown on page 32. Rapid increases in height during her admission to hospital and at boarding school were followed by stable linear growth. When she was 15 she ran away from home and her height eventually reached the 25th centile.

Further reading

Money J, Annecillo C, Kelley JF. Growth of intelligence; failure and catch-up associated respectively with abuse and rescue in the syndrome of abuse dwarfism. *Psychoneuroendocrinology* 1983;8:309–19.

Skuse D. The relationship between deprivation, physical growth and the impaired development of language. In: Fletcher P, ed. *Specific Speech and Language Disorders in Children*. London: Whurr Publications, 1992: 29–50.

Stanhope R, Adlard P, Hamill G, Jones J, Skuse D, Preece M. Physiological growth hormone (GH) secretion during the recovery from psychosocial dwarfism: a case report. *Clin Endocrinol (Oxf)* 1988;28:335–9.

Taitz LS, King JM. Growth patterns in child abuse. *Acta Paediatr Scand (Suppl)* 1988;343:62–72.

CHILD SEXUAL ABUSE–I

Frank Bamford, Raine Roberts

What is child sexual abuse?

Child sexual abuse is any use of children for the sexual gratification of adults.

Who abuses and who is abused?

The abuser is almost always a male known to the child: a relative (father, grandfather, uncle, or older brother); a member of the household (stepfather or mother's cohabitants); or a temporary carer—for example, teenage male babysitters. Note that abusing males may move after the discovery of abuse to another household of similar composition.

Child sexual abuse may occur in any part of society but is discovered more commonly in poor families.

Children of all ages and either sex may be sexually abused.

What happens?

Sexual abuse entails all types of sexual activity often with escalating intrusiveness.

Children may be exposed to indecent acts, pornographic photography, or external genital contact in the form of being fondled, masturbating an adult, or being used for intercrural intercourse. Finally, they may be penetrated orally, vaginally, or anally.

How often does sexual abuse occur?

Nobody knows how often sexual abuse occurs. It is certain that a lot of abuse is undiagnosed and equally certain that false diagnoses may be catastrophic.

Five main risk factors predispose to child sexual abuse.

● Previous incest or sexual deviance in the family
● New male member of the household with a record of sexual offences
● Loss of inhibition due to alcohol
● Loss of maternal libido or sexual rejection of father
● A paedophilic sexual orientation, especially in relation to sex rings and pornography.

Do children tell?

Sometimes children tell other people, but many are threatened to stop them telling. They may receive compensatory treats or presents.

Disclosure after a long period of abuse is common and may be followed by retraction. The statements of young children about sexual abuse should be taken seriously and, if possible, written down verbatim. Repeated questioning is potentially harmful and may evoke less truthful answers. Care is needed in understanding exactly what the child is saying—for example, "Daddy hurt my bum" may be interpreted in several ways, whereas "Daddy put his willie in my mouth" can hardly be anything other than abuse.

Does the non-abusing parent tell?

Sometimes the parent who is not sexually abusing the child will tell someone about the abuse, but collusion within families may occur, as in physical abuse. Beware of allegations made by parents in disputes about access or custody. Do not dismiss them but treat them with great caution.

How may sexual abuse present?

(1) Statements of the child.
(2) Symptoms due to local trauma or infection—for example, perineal soreness, vaginal discharge, and anal pain or bleeding.
(3) Symptoms attributable to emotional effects—for example, loss of concentration, enuresis, encopresis, anorexia, and parasuicide. A change in behaviour is important.
(4) Sexualised conduct or inappropriate sexual knowledge for young children. Remember that such conduct or knowledge may be derived from observing others or from pornographic videos, but if a child describes pain or the quality of semen, physical interference is probable.

What should be recorded?

Doctors dealing with child sexual abuse should keep a record of who asked them to see the child, who accompanied him or her, who raised the question of sexual abuse, who gave the history, and who was present at the examination.

The history should include details of the incident(s) causing suspicion; a full paediatric history, with particular emphasis on genitourinary or bowel symptoms; and details of previous abuse or sexual offences within the family or household.

Should the child be examined and where?

The child should be examined but not without the knowledge and agreement of a parent (or the order of a court). Mothers of preadolescent children should always be invited to be present, except in the most exceptional circumstances. Adolescent patients should be asked whether they wish a parent to be present.

It is usually counterproductive to examine a resistant child, and if his or her cooperation cannot be obtained the examination should be deferred unless there are urgent medical reasons to proceed.

The child should be examined as soon as optimal arrangements can be made. Few children require urgent examination.

Repetitive examination is usually abusive and should be avoided.

The examination should be conducted in absolute privacy and in an environment where the child can be comfortable—not behind screens in open wards or in police stations.

There should be adequate equipment for any necessary diagnostic tests. Recording and photographic facilities are an advantage but their value is outweighed if they cause distress to the child or mean that another examination has to be conducted.

Who should examine?

A person with skill in paediatric examination who is familiar with normal genital and anal appearances of children should conduct the examination. When physical abnormalities are expected from the history a forensic physician should be invited to examine or to be present during the examination so that it need not be repeated and a second opinion is available in doubtful cases.

Who should be present?

The only people present at the examination should be the child, his or her parent, and the examiner(s)—no one else—except, with the agreement of the parents, an occasional observer in training.

What about acute sexual abuse?

When abuse is thought to have been recent (within 72 hours) or there is serious genital injury forensic evidence must not be compromised. Examination should be deferred, if consistent with safety, until a forensic physician can be present. Nobody should remove clothing or attempt to clean or bath the child. Junior medical staff should not examine suspected victims unless the child urgently needs medical attention.

CHILD SEXUAL ABUSE–II

Frank Bamford, Raine Roberts

In child sexual abuse genital and anal examination should be in the context of a general clinical examination and include a search for other forms of abuse and an appraisal of growth, development, and health. The behaviour of the child in the presence of his or her parent should be noted.

Why should the genitalia be examined?

The genitalia should be examined in child sexual abuse for five main reasons.

- To detect traumatic or infective conditions that may require treatment
- To evaluate the nature of any abuse. Normal genital and anal appearances do not exclude the diagnosis, but in young children they make penetrative abuse unlikely
- To provide forensic evidence that may be helpful to the future protection of children
- To reassure the child, who sometimes feels that serious damage has been done
- To start the process of recovery.

How to examine the genitalia and anus

Cooperation during an examination is best achieved by telling children exactly what is happening and allowing them to feel in control by asking them to help. Let them take the swabs if they wish. The child may lie on her back for vulval inspection or on her side as for anal examination. With children up to 7 years old it is sometimes better for them to lie along the length of their mother's knee, facing forwards, with the mother gently flexing and abducting the hips. Adequate inspection requires a relaxed child.

Should fingers or a speculum be inserted?

Glaister's rods, if used gently in a cooperative child, may assist inspection of the edge of the hymen vaginalis but they are not absolutely necessary.

Some doctors insert a finger to assess the tone of the anal sphincter but unless there are clear indications of abuse it should be avoided. Views differ as to its importance.

In a small number of cases in which vaginal examination or repair is necessary the child should be given a general anaesthetic. General anaesthesia should also be considered if there

is vaginal bleeding after suspected abuse.

Can sexual abuse be proved by clinical examination?

Semen or blood of a group different from that of the child would, if present within the vagina or rectum or on the perineum in a prepubertal child, be conclusive evidence of interference, but such cases are uncommon in forensic practice and wholly exceptional in paediatric practice. Lubricants or hairs are of similar importance. Genital infection with *Neisseria gonorrhoeae* is indicative of contact with an infected person in 98% of cases, but all other findings can be produced by circumstances or conditions other than sexual abuse. It follows that, with the exceptions mentioned, the concept of a single, conclusive diagnostic sign is invalid.

How patent is a child's vagina?

The likelihood or otherwise of penetration may be inferred from the size of the hymenal orifice. Individual hymens vary substantially from the imperforate to the congenitally absent, and the hymen may occasionally be cribriform. In most prepubescent children it is a membrane with a circular or crescentic opening and a smooth, regular margin that may be either thin or rounded.

The diameter is difficult to measure accurately, but in most young children the unstretched hymenal orifice is no more than 0·5–0·6 cm, increasing slightly as puberty approaches. Rarely, the size of the hymenal orifice may be greater in normal prepubertal children. As the diameter of an adult index finger is about 1·5 cm and that of an erect penis two or three times greater, penetration is very unlikely to have occurred if there is an intact, unstretched hymen.

It is important to spend some time carefully observing the hymen before coming to any conclusion about it. A hymen appearing small and undamaged will sometimes open up as the child relaxes and tears and bumps may be seen. Gentle traction of the labia majora forwards and downwards may help to display the hymen more clearly and will make the orifice appear larger. The measurements with and without traction together with a diagram of the shape of the hymen should be recorded.

Child sexual abuse—II

Right: Tear of hymen, left lateral, would have been missed without use of Glaister's rod

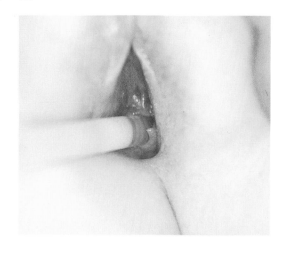

common in other conditions—for example, enuresis and poor hygiene. The rounded labia contour may be flattened, but it is not a reliable sign as flattening can be due to tight clothing. There may be a split of the posterior fourchette and a subsequent scar. Finally, the pressure of a penis against the hymen may stretch it and the child may think that there has been penetration.

What causes irregularity or tearing of the hymen?

The hymen may be damaged in four main ways.

- By sexual abuse
- By genital disease. A careful history is important
- By self injury. This is unusual because it is painful, but damage to the hymen may occur by the insertion of foreign bodies
- By accidental injury. This is also unusual because after infancy the introitus is protected by the labia.

Signs of intercrural intercourse

There are usually no signs of intercrural intercourse but occasionally bruising of the perineum may occur. It may cause patchy redness on the labia and perineum, but this is

Below left: Be careful not to mistake vestibule for hymen. On left vestibule is seen while middle picture (closer picture of same child) shows red crescent of hymen

Far right: Lichen sclerosus et atrophicus. Characteristic depigmentation of the labia majora extending to the anus. (Commonly there is wrinkling of the skin of the labia, from atrophy, and sometimes bruising or bleeding)

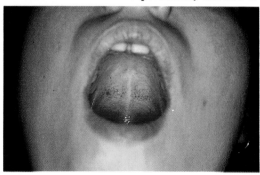

Petechial bruising on palate. Always look in mouth for signs of oral sex

Signs of buggery

The signs of buggery are likely to be most prominent in young children. In many cases there are no abnormal signs but look for evidence of external trauma, skin changes, and anal dilatation.

External trauma in anal abuse

Fissures due to overstretching of the sphincter are often multiple and radiate. Their extent is probably in proportion to the disparity in size between the assailant and the child and the degree of force used, and they may leave scars and sometimes anal skin tags. Be careful to distinguish fissures from prominent folds in the anal canal.

Swelling of the skin around the anal verge may be seen occasionally after recent abuse and thickening after repeated abuse. The skin of the anal verge may become rounded and smooth. Distinguish from lichen sclerosus et atrophicus (figure), perianal moniliasis, and scratching by children infected with threadworms. Skin changes by themselves are not sufficient to lead to investigation of abuse.

Perineal bruising or bleeding without reasonable explanation raises substantial suspicion. It must be distinguished from haemangiomata and dilated vessels. Veins may be dilated in association with bowel disorder.

Warts around the anus (or vaginal introitus) may be transmitted by genital contact. They are strongly suggestive of sexual abuse, especially if a wart virus of a genitally transmitted type is identified. Genital warts are usually smaller than common warts and appear as multiple papules along the inner surface of the labia or circumferentially around the anus. They occur particularly where skin is moist. Parents or children who have common warts

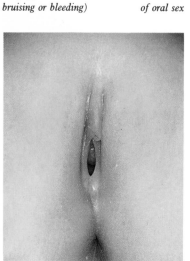

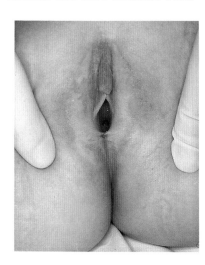

on their hands may infect skin in the region of the genitalia or anus during toileting.

Anal dilatation

Given that the bowel is normal and that the child does not suffer from any neurological disorder, abnormal patency is indicative of something hard and large having passed through the anus, but it is impossible to be sure whether the object has passed upwards or come downwards. A history of bowel problems or of medical investigation or treatment is therefore important. "Reflex" anal dilatation is not a true reflex. It amounts to relaxation of the anal sphincter about 10 seconds after the anus has been inspected so that an initially closed anus opens during the course of examination (alternatively an anus open at first closes during the examination and then opens again).

VARIATIONS IN HYMEN

Right: Two holes in hymen

Far right top: Septate hymen. Bands are usually vertical. Hymenal tags (not shown) may be incomplete bands and be mistaken for scars

Far right below: Bump on hymen. Hymen has probably been torn posteriorly leaving bumps and slight thickening

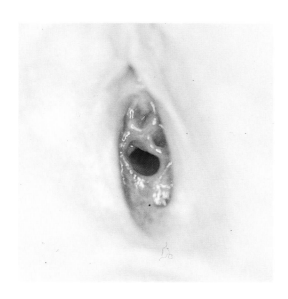
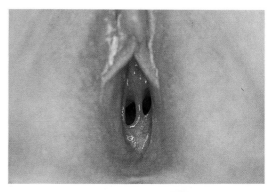
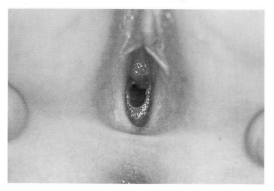

CLASSIC INJURY OF ATTEMPTED PENILE PENETRATION

Right: Haematoma of hymen and split of posterior fourchette

Far right: Recently torn hymen in teenage girl. Hymen usually tears in posterior half

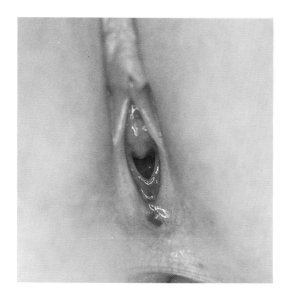
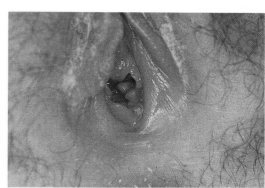

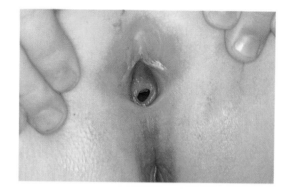

Inflamed, thickened hymen, in this case caused by rubbing

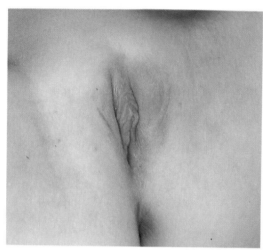

Redness caused by rubbing

Anal closure and continence is dependent upon the internal anal sphincter. If it is incompetent because of stretching or injury there is likely to be soiling. The internal anal sphincter may be relaxed physiologically by faeces in the lower rectum. In examining children in whom abuse is suspected it is important to ensure that they are relaxed, that the rectum is empty, and that there is no other source of pressure on it. When the internal sphincter is incompetent the external sphincter may be able to maintain closure for a short time but cannot sustain it, hence the changes seen during examination. "Reflex" anal dilatation may be a pointer to sexual abuse but is not reliable as a sole diagnostic sign and its significance is currently unproved.

Should tests be done for sexually transmitted disease?

Sexually transmitted disease should always be tested for in children molested by strangers. In intrafamilial cases obtain swabs unless it is clearly going to cause distress. Sometimes it is helpful to get suspected abusing parents to attend a genitourinary medicine clinic.

Taking a low vaginal swab at the initial examination may enable a presumptive diagnosis of gonorrhoea by Gram staining of a smear, but definitive diagnosis depends on culture and selective tests. If contact has been recent, a repeat swab will be needed because the incubation period of gonorrhoea is two to seven days. Swabs should also be taken from the pharynx and rectum.

Chlamydia trachomatis may cause asymptomatic infection. It can be detected by culture but this is not always available. If it is available special swabs and transport medium should be used. Enzyme immunoassay and direct immunofluorescent antibody tests are available but are not reliable. Interpretation of positive cultures in young children is difficult because the source of infection cannot easily be defined and the diagnostic value in relation to child sexual abuse is doubtful.

If herpetic lesions are seen on the genitalia a swab of fluid from the base of a lesion should be obtained and placed in virus transport medium for subsequent culture. Specimens can be stored at 4°C if any delay is anticipated. Recent typing techniques may enable matching with samples from a suspected abuser.

Trichomonas vaginalis is very uncommon in prepubertal children after the neonatal period because of vaginal alkalinity, but in post-pubertal children microscopic examination of vaginal secretion in a drop of physiological saline may reveal mobile flagellate organisms. Culture is also possible using appropriate media.

It is now very uncommon in Britain to see children with clinical signs of syphilis. The infection is excluded by appropriate serological tests immediately and three months after the last possible abusive contact.

ANAL DILATATION

Right: Place hands gently on buttocks and wait

Far right: Both sphincters open. Do not pull with fingers as false positive results will occur. Ensure rectum is empty. (Note that faeces can be seen in this girl's rectum)

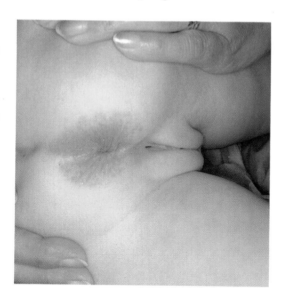

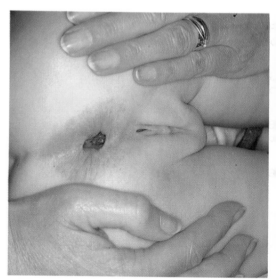

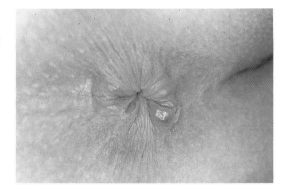

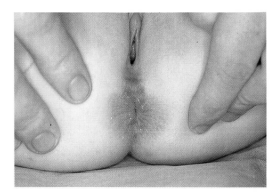

Buggery: Top pictures show swelling, bruising, and fissures of anal margin caused by recent buggery

Right: Anal dilatation, bruising, and fissure

Far right: Appearance of healed anus 10 days later

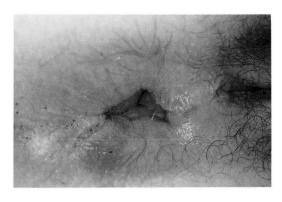

Tests for antibodies to HIV may be required later in specific cases, as may pregnancy tests in post-pubertal girls.

Medical management

The medical management of child sexual abuse is part of an interdisciplinary process. Communication with other agencies is essential.

Possible sexual abuse

(1) If child sexual abuse is only a possibility—for example, the child has made a vague statement, there are behavioural changes, vulval or anal soreness, or family risk factors—take a careful history from the carer and write down anything said by the child but do not engage in an intrusive interview.

(2) If the history points to a probability of abuse refer the child to an experienced person.

(3) If the history is not clearly indicative of abuse examine the whole child, including the genitalia, and take swabs if appropriate.

(4) Discuss the case with colleagues in the practice, including health visitors and possibly school nurses. Hospital doctors should discuss the case with the family's general practitioner. Some regions have experienced staff who are willing to advise. Ascertain whether the family is known by or has caused concern to the social services.

(5) Tell the carer of your findings and opinion.

(6) Arrange follow up visits and ensure that appointments are kept.

Probable sexual abuse

(1) If child sexual abuse is probable because of a clear statement from the child or unexplained recent vaginal or anal injury

*Genital and anal findings which **may** indicate abuse*

Redness or swelling of clitoris

Stretching or tearing of hymen

Bumps or irregularities of hymen

Bands or synechiae

Adhesions of labia minora

Splits or scarring of posterior fourchette

Perianal or perivulval warts

Perineal or perianal bruising or petechiae

Fissures and scars

Lax sphincter Dilatation

Skin changes due to rubbing

41

Treatment of cases of child sexual abuse by primary care doctors

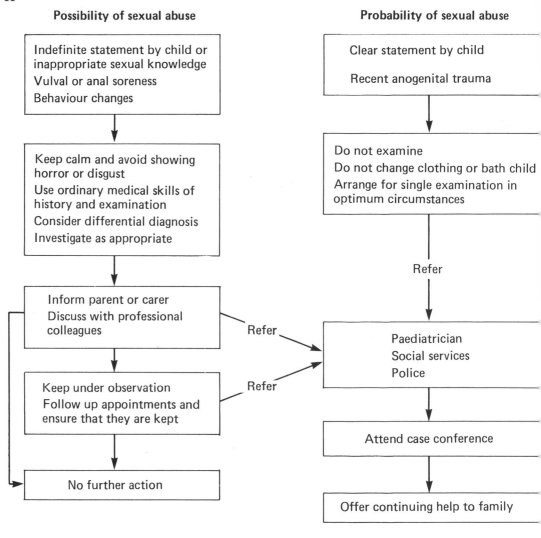

Possibility of sexual abuse

> Indefinite statement by child or inappropriate sexual knowledge
> Vulval or anal soreness
> Behaviour changes

> Keep calm and avoid showing horror or disgust
> Use ordinary medical skills of history and examination
> Consider differential diagnosis
> Investigate as appropriate

> Inform parent or carer
> Discuss with professional colleagues

> Keep under observation
> Follow up appointments and ensure that they are kept

> No further action

Probability of sexual abuse

> Clear statement by child
> Recent anogenital trauma

> Do not examine
> Do not change clothing or bath child
> Arrange for single examination in optimum circumstances

Refer

> Paediatrician
> Social services
> Police

> Attend case conference

> Offer continuing help to family

Refer

inform the police and social services department promptly, with the knowledge and, if possible, the agreement of the carer.

(2) Do not examine the child—arrange for a full, single paediatric and forensic examination at which suitable samples and photographs can be obtained.

(3) Check that the medical welfare of the child has been safeguarded—that is, infections treated and, if appropriate, pregnancy tests and postcoital contraception provided.

(4) Facilitate interviews of the child by a psychiatrist, psychologist, police officer, or social worker agreed by all the parties concerned. Avoid further abuse of the child by preventing different people going over the same material repetitively.

(5) Ascertain whether there are other children at risk and arrange to examine them.

(6) Participate in a multidisciplinary case conference.

(7) Ensure long term follow up with child psychiatrists as appropriate.

Allegations by an adult against another

When an adult accuses another adult of child sexual abuse refer the case to an experienced person because such cases often lead to litigation.

Violent sexual assault outside the family

Refer all cases in which children are violently assaulted outside the family to the police.

Do not touch or examine the child, except in an emergency.

Ensure the medical welfare of the child as in other cases but after forensic examinations are complete. Almost all victims require skilled psychiatric help.

Confidentiality

The overriding duty is to the child. It is usually possible to obtain the consent of one parent to examination and disclosure—in any event you are obliged to make sure that the parent(s) understand that information will be shared.

Further reading

Bays J, Chadwick D. Medical diagnosis of the sexuality abused child. *Child Abuse Negl* 1993;**17**:91–110.
Ciba Foundation. Porter R, ed. *Child sexual abuse within the family*. London: Tavistock, 1987.
De Jong A, Finkel MA. Sexual abuse of children. *Curr Probl Paediatrics* 1990;**20**:489–567.
Department of Health and Social Security. *Diagnosis of child sexual abuse: guidance for doctors*. London: HMSO, 1988.
Jones DPH, Lanning KV, Putnam FW. Three commentaries on ritualism and child sexual abuse. *Child Abuse Negl* 1991;**15**:163–7.
Royal College of Physicians. *Physical signs of sexual abuse in children*. London: RCP, 1991.

MUNCHAUSEN SYNDROME BY PROXY

Roy Meadow

RAISING THE COLLEGE OF PHYSICIANS

Baron von Munchausen, born in 1720, was a German mercenary and a gifted raconteur. Richard Asher in 1951 dedicated the Munchausen syndrome to the memory of the baron because the patients had his characteristic of travelling widely and telling false stories.

The picture shows Baron von Munchausen raising the College of Physicians of London into the air for three months (during which the health of its patients was never better)

Munchausen syndrome by proxy was used first in 1977 to describe children whose mothers invented stories of illness about their child and substantiated the stories by fabricating false physical signs.

The Munchausen syndrome is applied to adults who invent false stories of illness about themselves, thereby incurring needless investigations and treatments. For children affected by the Munchausen syndrome by proxy the proxy is the mother, who provides the false information. Child abuse results partly from the direct actions of the mother—for example, giving drugs to make the child unconscious—and partly from those of doctors, who arrange invasive investigations or needless treatment for a child at the mother's instigation.

In the past 10 years the boundaries of this type of abuse have been found to be wide and to overlap with other forms of abuse, and with the normal ways that families react when their child is ill. The abuse manifests itself in four main ways: perceived illness, doctor shopping, enforced invalidism, and fabricated illness.

Perceived illness

Anxious parents may worry needlessly that their healthy child is ill. A mother who is inexperienced, under stress, lonely, or herself ill is all the more likely to perceive symptoms in her child that others do not observe. The child is taken to doctors, perhaps on many occasions, if she cannot be reassured. Often the child will have unpleasant investigations and treatments because of the mother's insistence. Most doctors, however, would not classify this as child abuse unless the mother's persistence and refusal to accept normal results was excessive and the quality of the child's life was being seriously impaired.

Doctor shopping

Some parents shop around or seek help from a succession of different doctors. They may do this within the NHS or privately by paying for consultations. They persist in claiming that their healthy child is ill, and as each doctor in turn refuses further investigation they consult yet another doctor. The result for the child is a series of repetitive investigations and unpleasant venepunctures and a body that has been thoroughly irradiated and biopsied.

When a parent's conviction about illness reaches these delusional proportions it results in child abuse.

Enforced invalidism

Some parents who have an ill or disabled child seek to keep the child ill, increase the degree of disability, or ensure that the child is regarded as incapacitated (when he or she is not). Thus the parents of a child with normal intelligence who has difficulty with spelling may insist that their child is mentally disabled and persuade the education authorities to accept the child into a special school. Alternatively, parents of children with a mild hemiplegia may insist that they spend their time in a wheelchair and bring them up to believe that they cannot walk, when they can.

The link with school refusal and school phobia is obvious. In many cases the child is being brought up to believe that he or she is ill and to miss school. Normally when a child is absent from school for an extended time the education authorities have the power to force the parents to return the child to education, but the difficulty for the education authorities is that these children have a genuine medical problem and the parents can persuade the education authorities that the disability from the child's illness is greater than it is; home teaching or a special school may then be arranged.

Dealing with perceived illness, doctor shopping and enforced invalidism

When dealing with perceived illness, doctor shopping, or enforced invalidism the doctor should bear in mind that these types of behaviour are an extension of the usual way that many parents behave when their child is ill. As with all forms of child abuse, it is the degree of abuse that matters. For a worried parent to seek a second or third specialist opinion is reasonable: to seek a 22nd opinion is not. As doctors, we have to listen carefully to parents' worries and to believe them when they say that their child is ill. We have to work within the framework of parents' expectations and experience of health to help them to come to understand and accept their child's behaviour and health. No one will blame a mother who keeps her child away from school an extra day or two because her child has a chronic illness or disability. Most of us accept the strategies that parents adopt to deal with chronic illness within their family, even when we do not agree with them: if the mother believes that a special diet will lessen the number of seizures of the epileptic child then it is unreasonable to interfere unless the diet is definitely nutritionally unsound or very inconvenient. If the child is being forced to sleep on the back of an upturned cupboard enclosed in aluminium foil to avoid suspected allergens, however, the strategy amounts to child abuse and interference is necessary.

With such families early cooperation with health visitors and also social services may be helpful. For hospital doctors close consultation with the general practitioner is needed because only the general practitioner may be aware of the many other specialists previously consulted. If the parents cannot be dissuaded by careful and sympathetic help from their perceptions and actions that are harming their child then child abuse procedures should be invoked.

Fabricated illness

Fabricated or factitious illness results from parents who lie to the doctor about their child's health and from those who fabricate physical signs or alter health records. Some parents do all these things, but it can be equally serious for the child if the parent merely relates persistently and realistically a convincing history of illness—for example, many epileptic seizures each week—for the story alone will cause the doctor to embark on detailed investigations and prescribe anticonvulsant treatment. Parents invent the false illness while the child is young—usually starting within the first two years. They may continue and intensify the story of illness as the years pass. If the deception is not uncovered before the child is of school age some children will participate in the deception. The mother teaches the child to trick the doctors and to lie. Some children subsequently have become independent illness addicts and have grown up to have the Munchausen syndrome.

There are five main consequences for chidren who are falsely labelled as ill.

(1) They will receive needless and harmful investigations and treatments.

(2) A genuine disease may be induced by the mother's actions—for example, renal failure as a result of regular injections of immunisation agents given to cause fever.

(3) They may die suddenly as a result of the mother misjudging the degree of insult. Mothers who, for example, partially suffocate their children to cause unconsciousness may smother the child for too long thereby causing brain damage or death.

(4) They may develop chronic invalidism. The child accepts the illness story and believes himself to be disabled and unable to attend school, to work, or even to walk.

(5) They may develop Munchausen syndrome as an adult—the children have learnt and then taken over the lying behaviour of their mother.

The stories of false illness usually concern the common chronic disorders of childhood: recurrent seizures, diarrhoea and vomiting, rashes, allergy, and fevers. Often they include more dramatic items such as recurrent bleeding.

In many instances the mother confirms the false history with false signs. The table lists some false signs together with the usual ways in which they are caused. In the more serious cases the mother harms the child directly—for example, by poisoning or suffocation—to cause the child to be ill. Commonly such direct harm is preceded by a period of false stories which have caused indirect harm to the child.

The consequences may be serious: some children have been in hospital for more than 18 months, during which their mothers have continued to lie and to fabricate signs; others have been absent from school for more than two years or have had lengthy periods of parenteral feeding, intravenous drug treatments, and inappropriate surgery.

In nearly all cases the mother is the

Fabricated illnesses

False sign	Cause
Seizures, apnoea, and drowsiness	Poisons, suffocation, pressure on neck
Bleeding (haematuria, haematemesis, etc)	Blood from mother (particularly vaginal tampon), raw meat, or from child, added to sample from child or smeared around child's nose, vulva, etc Colouring agents added to sample or smeared on to child Warfarin administration
Fever	Warming thermometer Altering temperature chart Injections of contaminated material into child's vein Repetitive injections of antigenic material
Diarrhoea	Laxatives
Vomiting	Mechanically induced Salt or emetic poisoning
Hypertension	Altering blood pressure chart or instructions concerning size of cuff for blood pressure estimation
Rashes	Scratching the skin to cause blisters Caustics and dyes
Renal stone	Addition of stone to child's urine to which blood has previously been added
Faeculent vomits	Making child vomit and stirring in faeces
Failure to thrive and thinness	Withholding food If in hospital and child is parenterally fed interfering with treatment and sucking back stomach contents through nasogastric tube

Action on suspicion of factitious illness

- Check history in detail—obtain verification of events alleged to have occurred in presence of third parties
- Seek temporal association between events and mother's presence
- Check personal, social, and family history—often the mother will have lied about them
- Contact other family members and doctors or health workers concerned
- Seek a motive—What is the mother gaining from making her child ill?

In hospital

- Secure and verify charts and records
- Retain and analyse samples—for example, blood and urine samples for toxicology
- Increase surveillance
- Participate with social services
- Exclude mother (aim for voluntary exclusion, though legal enforcement may be required)

deceiver: the father does not know what is going on. The mother tends to be the dominant person in the marriage and to be more intelligent and capable than her husband. The husband tends to be in the background getting on with his own life and unsupportive of his wife's needs. In the small minority (less than 5%) of cases in which the father is the perpetrator the roles are reversed and the father tends to be the dominant person in the marriage and the mother unaware and unbelieving of the abuse. Similarly rare are cases in which another carer—for example, a nurse—is the perpetrator.

The mothers have often had a difficult childhood themselves and have usually lacked love and respect from their own mothers; many have been abused as children. As they have grown up it is common for them to have worked as nurses, care assistants, or in other occupations concerned with health. Nearly a quarter of the mothers have somatoform behaviour and are personal illness addicts; some are notorious in their neighbourhood for presenting with unexplained illnesses and might be classified as having Munchausen syndrome themselves.

The mothers usually stay with one general practitioner and, when referred to hospital, with one specialist. The child's referral to other specialists comes from the general practitioner or the hospital specialist. For the more complicated cases the children are transferred from one centre of excellence to another, where they undergo repetitive examination. The mother thrives on this, accompanying the child to the different hospitals, and is an avid consumer of good facilities for resident mothers.

Although many of the mothers may have had contact with psychiatrists in the past, it is unusual for them to have had previous mental illness or to be found to have such illness at

the time of the abuse. On formal testing most do have personality disorders with histrionic, dependent and borderline personalities being identified most commonly.

Warning signs

In nearly half the families other siblings are suffering (or have suffered) similar abuse or another variety of abuse, and in a few families there has been unexplained death of other young children.

Groups of children who are particularly likely to include some with factitious illness are those receiving intensive treatment for severe allergy or recurrent apnoea and those receiving parenteral feeding (particularly when the treatment or care has to be intensified to an unusual degree in a child for whom objective tests have been relatively normal).

It is important to recognise that some of the victims will have genuine illness in addition to the superimposed false illness. Moreover, up to a third of the children will have, or have had, failure to thrive, non-accidental injury, or neglect in addition to the factitious illness abuse.

Some of the warning signs that should alert a doctor to fabricated illness are listed below.

(1) The illness is unexplained, prolonged, or extremely rare.

(2) The symptoms and signs have a temporal association with the mother's presence. They may also be incongruous—for example, blood stained vomit from a child who is pink and laughing and has a full volume pulse.

(3) The mother is a hospital addict and more anxious to impress the doctor than she is worried about her child's illness.

(4) The treatment prescribed is ineffective and not tolerated.

(5) In the family there are multiple illnesses and similar symptoms in other members.

Motive

The motives vary. For most mothers there is personal gain in terms of status; contacts with helpful doctors, nurses, and social workers; financial benefits; contact with other mothers and a different society in hospital; escape from an unhappy marriage; or the capture of an absent husband to share a problem. The mothers seem to be able to do horrific things to their child because of their own unhappiness and to satisfy their own needs. With suffocation or poisoning there is commonly envy of, and violence and hatred towards, the abused child.

Action and reaction

At one end of its range fabricated illness is as serious as any other type of abuse and calls for prompt liaison with social services, and sometimes the police, to protect the child. It is, however, important not to overreact just because a mother is lying or fabricating signs. Sometimes a mother may add blood to her child's urine or alter a temperature chart to dissuade the doctors from discharging her child from hospital before she is sufficiently reassured and ready to cope. Such minor events are common and should be sorted out sympathetically and promptly in a way that dissuades the mother from giving false histories or fabricating signs again.

The doctor discovering deception has to stand back for a moment and work out exactly how much the child is being harmed by the mother's direct and indirect actions and then discuss those factors with the social services.

Further reading

Bools CN, Neale BA, Meadow SR. Comorbidity associated with fabricated illness (Munchausen syndrome by proxy). *Arch Dis Child* 1992;**62**:77–9.

Meadow R. Management of Munchausen syndrome by proxy. *Arch Dis Child* 1985;**60**:385–93.

Meadow R. Munchausen syndrome by proxy. *Arch Dis Child* 1982;**57**:92–8.

Neale B, Bools C, Meadow R. Problems in the assessment and management of Munchausen syndrome by proxy abuse. *Children and Society* 1991;**5**:324–33.

Rosenberg DA. Web of deceit: a literature review of Munchausen syndrome by proxy. *Child Abus Negl* 1987;**11**:547–63.

Waller DA. Obstacles to the treatment of Munchausen by proxy syndrome. *Journal of the American Academy of Child Psychiatry* 1983;**22**:80–5.

ROLE OF THE CHILD PSYCHIATRY TEAM

Ingrid Davison, Rory Nicol

Child psychiatrists' training in adult mental health and often, nowadays, in paediatrics as well as their experience of the development and emotional, behavioural, and social functioning of children places them in a unique position in medicine. They work in different settings across the country, but most work within a multidisciplinary team, which may include a clinical psychologist, educational psychologist, social worker, community psychiatric nurse, occupational therapist, specialist teacher, and non-medical child psychotherapist, as well as a consultant child psychiatrist. A child psychiatrist working with such a team is well placed to make a holistic assessment of a child and its family and to offer treatment accordingly.

Why should child psychiatrists become involved in child abuse?

All forms of child abuse will have a psychological impact on the child, and may affect his or her emotional, social, and behavioural adjustment, and development, and are therefore of interest to the child psychiatrist. Such effects may be short term or long term but are not inevitable. Well timed treatment will modify the later outcome of child abuse, but child psychiatrists are also aware of the importance of resilience factors in a child's life which can protect him or her against the full impact of adverse experiences.

Childhood experience	Possible outcome
Understimulation	Developmental delays
Emotional neglect	Indiscriminate overfriendliness, overactivity, and aggression
	Problems in making and sustaining intimate personal relationships
Emotional abuse	Disturbed feeding behaviour, wetting, and soiling
	Poor social adjustment
	Antisocial behaviour
Excessive punitiveness	Passive "frozen" behaviour
	Disorganized aggression
Family violence	Conduct disorder
Sexual abuse	Sexualised behaviour
	Self mutilation
	Eating disorders
	Depression
	Sexual dysfunction

It is important to identify positive features in a child's experience as well as negative ones when predicting future outcome.

The box below simplifies some of the adverse emotional and behavioural effects associated with child abuse, together with possible potential outcomes in later childhood and adult life.

When should the child psychiatrist become involved in cases of child abuse?

There are several points in the management of child abuse when involvement of the child psychiatry team should be considered. A child psychiatrist is particularly likely to be helpful when he or she has extensive experience of this difficult work.

Investigation

It is helpful for child psychiatrists to become involved early in cases of child abuse. However, the role of identification is primarily one for the police and social services departments. In more complex cases the expertise of the child psychiatrist will be of assistance in understanding the relationship of behaviour, emotions, and family problems with potential abuse.

Assessment

Not all cases of proven child abuse require assessment by the child psychiatric team. If the child is coping well at home and at school and has a supportive relationship with a caring adult, further intervention might be counterproductive.

An assessment by a child psychiatrist is indicated if the children in the family are presenting with emotional, behavioural, or social difficulties or a delay in development. The child psychiatrist's training and experience is such that he or she is well equipped to assess in addition parental mental health, the nature of family relationships, and, most importantly, the quality of parenting provided to the children.

In cases where there is doubt about child abuse the child psychiatrist should still be involved if there is concern about the emotional, social, and behavioural adjustment and development of the child. He or she may be able to shed useful light on the probability of child abuse having occurred, which can then be investigated further by the appropriate agencies. This is particularly so when emotional abuse is suspected. Emotional abuse is defined as "the severe adverse effect on the behaviour and emotional development of a child caused by persistent or severe emotional ill treatment or rejection." Its diagnosis therefore falls squarely within the clinical remit of the child psychiatrist, who should be able to provide valuable insights into the nature and effect of such abuse.

Court work

The Children Act 1989 has placed a new emphasis on the multidisciplinary assessment of children and their families and has placed an obligation on health authorities to cooperate in such assessments. This is likely to lead to increased demands by the courts on child psychiatrists to assess and formulate problems of child abuse within families and to advise on future management and treatment. All child psychiatrists should have expertise in presenting complex problems in a way that can be understood by the court.

Management

Information is needed in a variety of areas if correct decisions are to be made. These include information about the nature, severity, and effect of the abuse; the risk of continuing abuse; the quality of parenting; the quality of family relationships; and the family's potential for change. The balance between the risks of continuing abuse if the child remains with its family and the inevitable damage resulting from removal from the family must be assessed. Long term plans about child care must be made as quickly as possible and must ensure that the best interests of the child are paramount. In practice, this often means deciding which is the least damaging of several alternatives.

The training and experience of a child psychiatrist familiar with such cases can be invaluable in this decision making process. Child psychiatrists should play a part in case conferences and meetings, planning the long term management of cases in which they have become involved. This role has received new emphasis in judgments given in recent well publicised child sexual abuse cases.

In addition to collaborating in the long term management of child abuse cases, the child psychiatrist is in a good position to advise about specific treatment and management.

Treatment

It is generally accepted that the major role of the child psychiatry team in cases of child abuse is in the provision of treatment. The focus of treatment must be the welfare of the child and the improvement of parent–child relationships, even if the child is not the identified patient in treatment. These concepts may be unfamiliar to professionals who do not work regularly with abused children. Since treatment programmes are often individually tailored, it is impossible to describe all possible

approaches. However, the following are particularly relevant to child abuse.

● Occasionally parental mental illness contributes to the abuse of a child. While the child psychiatrist, with training in adult mental health as well as experience of child abuse and family functioning, is in a good position to diagnose such illness, it is advisable to involve the general adult psychiatric service in treatment. The adult psychiatrist should then also be involved in planning long term management of the case, since he or she will be able to advise about the likely outcome of treatment and have access to other resources, which may be helpful.

● More commonly it is not possible to diagnose a specific mental illness, but one or both parents may show evidence of a personality disorder associated with poor quality of parenting, and inadequate control of impulses. Psychological intervention aimed at enabling parents to assume responsibility for their behaviour and to control their impulses may be helpful. A number of different professionals might take on this work, but it is often helpful to involve the local forensic psychiatry service, who are especially experienced in this area.

● Assessment of abusive families often reveals a multigenerational cycle of abuse, with parents who have experienced abuse in their own childhoods then going on to repeat similar abuse with their own children. Often parents have spoken to no one about these experiences and, once having broached the issue, are keen to have help for themselves. In such situations a referral to the local adult psychotherapy or counselling service may be helpful. Alternatively it may be necessary for the professionals working with the family, including the child psychiatric team, to address these issues with the parents before they are able to move on and improve their parenting skills. The social workers who work with the child psychiatric team often have skills and expertise particularly relevant in this area.

● Improving parenting skills is clearly an important aim when working with abusive families, and can be tackled in a variety of different ways. Parents often need advice about behavioural management techniques. In abusing families the importance of praise and rewards for appropriate behaviour often need particular emphasis, as well as the use of non-abusive sanctions for undesirable behaviour. Some child psychiatric teams have day or inpatient resources where families are admitted for observation and modification of parenting skills on a here and now basis and the clinical psychologist in the team can be particularly helpful in devising appropriate programmes. In many areas such work is undertaken in family centres run by the local social services department. The child psychiatric team can offer support and consultation to such establishments.

• Abused children often present with serious and persistent emotional and behavioural problems which require treatment if future development is to proceed. In younger children play therapy is a valuable approach, allowing the child the opportunity to explore his or her feelings about the abuse through the medium of play. In older children individual psychotherapy is treatment based on talking, which addresses the same issues, although with all children drawing and play materials can add to the therapeutic process.

• Psychotherapy is hard work that requires motivation and inner strength on the part of the child. For some children it is not an appropriate treatment, particularly for those who have been severely damaged by their experiences or those whose future remains uncertain. For these children the child psychiatric team can still offer help by working with their carers, to enable them to offer understanding and support to the children in their daily lives.

• Sexually abused children may present with sexualised behaviour which leaves them vulnerable to further abuse. It is important to undertake work with these children that will enable them to protect themselves in the future. This work usually focuses on the child's rights over his or her own body, the difference between caring and abusive touching, good and bad secrets, and strategies that the child can use to escape from potentially abusive situations. These issues are often most successfully addressed among a group of developmentally similar children, but if a group is not available there is no reason why the work cannot be undertaken on an individual basis.

• Group approaches can be helpful in the treatment of child abuse. Protective groups for sexually abused children have already been mentioned, but parent training groups, play groups for abused children, groups for mothers of sexually abused children, and groups for perpetrators are all receiving increasing attention.

• Conjoint family approaches—that is, those in which the whole family is seen together—can be useful in physical, emotional, and sexual abuse but need to be used with caution and when the aim of the treatment is

clear. Their indiscriminate use by inexperienced therapists is naive and potentially damaging.

• Abuse carried out by children is receiving more recognition and is an important issue for child psychiatrists. Such children have often been abused themselves and have then gone on to abuse others. They must be helped to acknowledge responsibility for their own abusive actions and to begin to make reparation before they can then go on to explore their experiences of abuse. These children raise questions about accepted stereotypes of sexual abuse and are particularly challenging to work with.

These specific interventions should be subordinate to the overall treatment and management programme for the children and families. The process and results of treatment need to be carefully documented because, apart from the specific benefits of the treatment, they may contribute valuable information about the capacity and motivation of the family to change and hence contribute to the major multidisciplinary decisions that need to be made about the family at case conferences.

Consultation and education

Child abuse is a harrowing and disturbing aspect of modern life and not all professionals who come into contact with such cases have the training or experience to prepare them adequately. The child psychiatry team can be a useful local resource offering consultation and education to professionals in the specialty, either by means of formalised training programmes or consultation arrangements—for example, with residential children's homes or on an ad hoc case by case basis.

Further reading

Bentovim A, Elton A, Hilderbrand J, Tranter M, Vizard E, eds. *Child sexual abuse within the family: assessment and treatment.* Sevenoaks: Wright, 1988.
Black D, Wolkind S, Hendriks JH, eds. *Child psychiatry and the law.* London: Royal College of Psychiatrists, 1989.
Nicol AR. The treatment of child abuse in the home environment. In: Browne K, Davies C, Stratton P, eds. *Early prediction and prevention of child abuse.* Chichester: Wiley, 1988.
Working together under the Child Act 1989: A guide to arrangements for the inter-agency co-operaton for the protection of children from abuse. London: HMSO 1991.

SOCIAL WORKERS AND CHILD PROTECTION

Michael Preston-Shoot

Local authority social services departments have four major child protection duties arising from the Children Act 1989: to prevent children suffering ill treatment and neglect; to safeguard and promote the welfare of children in need; to investigate a child's circumstances when requested by a court; and (along with the National Society for the Prevention of Cruelty to Children (NSPCC)) to investigate information that a child is suffering or is likely to suffer significant harm and decide whether any action should be taken to safeguard and promote the child's welfare. Each local authority has its own procedures but must work within the definitions of significant harm, children in need, and health and development provided in the act and elaborated in subsequent guidance, much of which for social services departments has the full force of legislation.

Local authorities vary in their organisational structures. Sometimes social workers are based in community offices, allocating referred work to particular practitioners on the basis of geographical area served or specialism (such as short term or long term work; children and families or adult services). Some local authorities also maintain hospital social work departments, where practitioners work with nominated wards, medical specialties, or consultants. Local authorities vary in the extent to which, after referral and initial investigation, hospital social workers are involved in child protection cases.

In all work with children and families the child's welfare is paramount, and is determined by consideration of a welfare checklist (section 1(3) of the Children Act 1989). Social work practice operates within this framework, which seeks to balance parental responsibility and rights with children's rights and the duty of the State to intervene in certain circumstances. Five principles inform such practice.

Primacy of family—This entails promoting the upbringing of children in need by their families when consistent with the duty to safeguard and promote the child's welfare. Services may be provided to assist families—for instance, day care, family centres, and counselling. Courts will make orders only when satisfied that so doing would be better than making no order at all. Parents retain parental responsibility when a child is in care; the local authority is able to limit this only when necessary to safeguard and promote the child's welfare. Where practicable and appropriate children looked after by the local authority should be placed near home or within the extended family, or both.

Partnership—This is the most effective means of providing care for children, whatever the legal position. It means the full involvement of parents and children in assessment, decision making, and reviews. A key feature is the negotiation of written agreements which detail the purpose and content of the work to be done.

Multidisciplinary teamwork—No one professional group has all the knowledge and skills required for the prevention of abuse or neglect or for child protection. Social workers may request assistance from other professionals working with children and families, who must assist (sections 27 and 47(10), Children Act 1989) unless this is unreasonable or prejudicial to the discharge of their own functions. Area

Key practice skills

- Honesty and openness
- Providing information about the purposes of interviews and available services
- Clear explanations of local authority powers and duties, reasons for concern, and what is or is not negotiable about involvement
- Clear language and preparation with families to enable their informed participation in decision making
- Engaging with the expression of strong feelings without defensiveness
- Addressing conflicts of interest directly, working with the family without compromising the child's interests
- Listening to families, entering their world and understanding their perspective, without colluding with the family, becoming overwhelmed, or maintaining unrealistic optimism
- Planning and reviews, to avoid drift and to retain clear objectives
- Written agreements detailing the child's needs, the plan to meet these needs, the actions required by those involved, and the timescale
- Work tackles the family's concerns and develops, where possible, their skills and strengths
- Recording—a detailed individual and family history cross referenced with significant events; the content and process of investigation, assessment, decision making, and intervention
- Decisions confirmed in writing
- Self awareness—monitoring the interaction between self and work, especially defence mechanisms such as avoidance of issues, defensive practice, and authoritarianism

child protection committees are responsible for developing agreed objectives and procedures for interagency cooperation in case management and decision making. This is crucial since interagency dangerousness, disagreements, or conflicts between professionals undermine child protection work.

Antidiscriminatory practice—Local authority services and practice must not reflect or reinforce discrimination and must meet the special needs of particular groups (Race Relations Act 1976; Children Act 1989). Thus when making decisions about children race, culture, religion, and linguistic background must be considered. Moreover, social workers work to counteract the impact of discrimination arising from race, gender, disability, age, poverty, and sexual preference. Accordingly, work will target the impact of inequality and structural oppression on individuals and families. The power imbalance between clients and professionals will be challenged through the use of written agreements, client advocates, open records, informed participation in meetings, and attention to workers' gender and ethnicity.

Prevention—Legal options should be the least coercive consistent with meeting the child's needs, including no order at all. Compulsory orders (emergency protection, child assessment, care orders) should be sought for the following reasons.

- When they are better than voluntary arrangements—that is, when services have been refused or failed, or are likely to fail to promote the child's welfare; when there is serious risk; when assessment is frustrated
- When they are in the interests of the child—based on clearly identified needs
- After a detailed investigation and case conference which consider whether services by agreement with the family would meet the child's needs.

Emergency protection orders should not be the routine first step in response to child abuse except in situations of clear and serious risk of significant harm.

More broadly, social services departments will, through liaison with other agencies and community groups, seek to develop community networks and resources in order to reduce environmental pressures and promote the prevention of abuse or neglect and the protection of children.

Assessment and intervention

Within the framework of these key practice principles and skills, together with open discussion between professionals and with children and parents, minimising delay and avoiding unnecessary intervention which prejudice the child's welfare, and ongoing consideration of the child's safety, social work practice has six interlocking components.

Acquisition and collation of information through facilitative questions; observation; listening and clarification; informing decision making by placing risks to and needs of the child in the context of family history, significant events, and details of abuse or neglect. Social workers will follow the guidance given in the Cleveland report, interviewing at the child's pace, restricting the number of interviews, ensuring the suitability of the work setting, and recording carefully. Creation of a safe space (reliability, consistency, role clarity) is essential if those involved are to be enabled to provide information and to convey their feelings and experiences. Social workers will look for evidence which corroborates statements of abuse or neglect. They must avoid preconceptions and exerting undue influence on people to disclose.

Study and evaluation of information—This entails distinguishing fact from opinion and content (the "what") from process (how people have engaged with the issues), using research and theoretical knowledge, and considering the case from different perspectives. The task here is to understand and appraise the available information. For instance, what is the effect of parental behaviour on the child? What awareness is there in the family of the child's needs? What networks are available to support this family? How cooperative have the parents been with professionals?

Formulation of assessment—This entails defining and clarifying problems and weighing up risks, needs, and resources. A needs assessment focuses on the child and the family, with special reference to the child's health and development (physical and mental health and social, emotional, educational, physical, and behavioural development) and environmental stresses (housing, income, race, and social and community networks). Resource assessment includes those resources available to the family and those resources within the professional network which might enable risks to be

---

Risk assessment

By using agreed indicators of risk and levels of (significant) harm the objective is to determine the seriousness of risk and harm or the likelihood of risk and harm, or both. This must then be considered alongside possible interventions: balancing the effects of removing the child with the possibility of harm if not removed from home and whether a voluntary agreement with the parents is sufficient to safeguard the child's welfare.

● Low risk	Monitoring, with clear criteria when to
● Potential risk	act; ongoing assessment; negotiated
● Moderate risk	agreement sought on work to be done; legal options considered if agreement is not possible
● Cumulative risk	Legal options to protect the child considered; agreement sought on work to be done; ongoing assessment
● Acute/immediate risk	May warrant immediate removal of the child

Assessing prospects for rehabilitation

Checklists have been developed to identify families where the rehabilitation of abused children might be indicated. No checklist is foolproof. Care must be taken that they do not oppress families by the inappropriate imposition of white eurocentric norms and the exclusion of structural issues (such as racism, poverty, unemployment, and housing). Each case must be considered alongside the availability of research knowledge. However, checklists do emphasise the factors that must be included in this type of assessment:

- What was the nature, frequency, and severity of the abuse or neglect?

- Has the abuse stopped? Is there a culture of violence or aggression in the family? How are relationships and decisions managed? How is power used?

- Do the parents accept responsibility and the need for change? Can they work for this change?

- Is there open communication about the abuse or neglect and about family problems? Are there substantial family problems? To what extent are the parents able to meet the child's needs? Is there a distinction between the child's needs and parents' needs? Are expectations of children realistic?

- Can the child resist any abuse? Has the child available non-abusive supports?

- Have the child's views been sought, worked with, and considered? Is the child fearful or requesting protection? Is the child accommodating to the abusing or neglectful parent?

- What has been the outcome of previous work with the family, if any?

decreased, problems resolved, and needs met. An initial investigation and assessment will consider the sources and levels of risk or harm or both, and the grounds for concern, culminating in recommendations of how best to protect the child, including the legal options most likely to promote this. Where an investigation and assessment rule out abuse or neglect, everyone involved must be informed in writing and services offered to children in need and their families. A comprehensive assessment, when requested by a court or case conference to provide the basis for decisions about the future management of the case, will gather and evaluate information on the areas of concern: the child's health and development; the family's resources, strengths, and problems; family interactions and the ability to meet the child's needs; and available support networks. Again, recommendations will be made about what needs to change to reduce the risk to the child or meet his or her needs, or both, and what form of intervention is most likely to achieve this.

Child protection plan—A statement about the work's objectives and how these are to be achieved. These plans should include the child's needs (including education, health, and race); how these needs are to be met; services to be provided, including placements, with their aims and timescales; arrangements for contact between child and family; arrangements for consulting the child, parents, and significant others and how they are to be involved in decision making; responsibility for implementing the plan; contingency plans if the plan or placement breaks down; and review dates.

Intervention with individuals (child, non-abusing parent, perpetrator) or families, or both. Therapeutic work may entail play therapy with children, family therapy, or the use of group work with, say, survivors or perpetrators of abuse. The objectives of intervention may be to decrease risks of abuse or neglect, to improve an individual's or family's strengths and resources, or to work through the effects of abuse or neglect. Intervention, when a child has been removed from home, may aim to test the prospects for rehabilitation or, if return home has been excluded, to work towards a permanent placement. The first six weeks are crucial when considering rehabilitation or permanent placement if work is to remain focused and purposeful.

Review—This entails involving parents, children, and relevant other people involved in the case to evaluate progress achieved, to reconsider the child protection plan and whether any change is necessary in the child's legal status, and to establish the framework and content of forthcoming work to safeguard and promote the child's welfare. Written notification of the outcome must be given to those involved in the case. Reviews demonstrate that assessment is an ongoing process involving the child, family, and professional network.

Contact

The frequency and length of contact between social workers and families varies. During initial investigations it can be daily for several hours. When supervising meetings between children looked after by the local authority and their parents it can amount to several times each week over a considerable period. Contact during assessments is often weekly, with comprehensive assessments requiring between eight and 12 weeks. Frequency and length of contact at the intervention stage will vary considerably depending on the method and focus of the work. The volume of work is such that concerns exist that social workers are underresourced; in particular that the time involved in initial investigations, child protection assessments, recording, and court work limits resources for intervention after assessment or work with other client groups.

Further reading

Bentovim A, Elton A, Tranter M. Prognosis for rehabilitation after abuse. *Adoption and Fostering* 1987;**11**:26–31.
Braye S, Preston-Shoot M. *Practising social work law.* London: Macmillan, 1992.
Butler-Sloss E. *Report of the inquiry into child abuse in Cleveland.* London: HMSO, 1988.
Corby B, Mills C. Child abuse: risks and resources. *Br J Social Work* 1986;**16**:531–42.
Curnock K, Hardiker P. *Towards practice theory. Skills and methods in social assessments.* London: Routledge and Kegan Paul, 1979.
DHSS. *Child abuse: a study of inquiry reports, 1973–1981.* London: HMSO, 1982.

CASE CONFERENCES

Michael Preston-Shoot

Case conferences are central to assessment, interagency cooperation, and decision making in child protection. They are convened by social services departments (and sometimes the National Society for the Prevention of Cruelty to Children (NSPCC)) when an initial investigation has confirmed or suspected abuse or neglect. To be effective their decisions must follow from consideration of all the available information, including a detailed individual and family history, cross referenced with significant family events, and an appraisal of the family's ability to protect the child and willingness to cooperate with professionals.

Except in relation to registration and the appointment of a key worker, case conferences make recommendations to participant agencies. These agencies should follow locally agreed procedures for confirming their intention to implement these recommendations. The key worker will be a local authority or NSPCC social worker. He or she may not be the person most in contact with the family, but will ensure that the child protection plan is developed and implemented, and is central to interagency work: coordinating agency contributions to assessment, intervention, and review; engaging the child and parents in the child protection plan; and facilitating communication between agencies.

Confidentiality

Confidentiality is a key question since effective intervention and case management depend on consideration of all available information. Child protection inquiries commonly pinpoint the failure to disclose or ask for information crucial in distorting assessment and decision making.

Codes of confidentiality issued by the General Medical Council, the British Association of Social Workers, and the United Kingdom Central Council for Nursing, Midwifery and Health Visiting allow disclosure and confirm the duty to share information when there is reason to believe a person is being abused or that serious danger exists. The paramount duty is the protection of the child.

Composition of case conferences

Case conferences include those with specific child protection responsibilities and those with a contribution to make to the specific case.

Chairperson—This is a senior member of the social services department (occasionally the NSPCC), with detailed knowledge and understanding of child protection and without line management responsibility for the case now or previously. Where possible the same person should chair all case conferences concerning particular children and families. The chairperson ensures the conference prioritises the child's interests, clarifies the meeting's purpose and the roles of people present, and facilitates each person to contribute verbally and by reports.

NSPCC—Some staff attend as observers or consultants when not directly involved in the case. They may provide comprehensive assessments to inform decision making, or resources such as family centres and family therapy.

Social workers and team leader report on the initial investigation and provide background information; they are responsible for ensuring that everyone with a relevant contribution to make has been invited; and they collate and record all available information.

Education welfare officers are sometimes concerned directly in an investigation or able to provide information about the family, or both, especially the child's school attendance and performance.

Teachers, nursery and playgroup workers, and childminders often observe symptoms of abuse or neglect; they may be the first to whom a child discloses abuse.

Police will provide information on any suspected individual discussed at the conference and, where officers have been coworkers with social workers in the initial investigation, will report on their assessment after interviews with the child, parents, or

---

Tasks of case conferences

- To share and coordinate information and concerns about the child and family, to assess the severity of abuse and neglect, and to evaluate the degree of risk

- To fulfil statutory obligations for the protection of children

- To formulate an agreed, recommended plan of management and intervention that addresses the abuse or neglect, risks, and needs in the case, with the child's welfare and safety the paramount aim. This must include consideration of what legal action is necessary to protect the abused or neglected child and other children in the family and what services should be provided on the basis of assessed needs

- To decide whether to place the child's name on the child protection register (see pp 3 and 7) and to nominate a key worker

- To agree if and when a child protection review is required—no more than six months from the initial case conference when the child's name has been placed on the register

---

Case conferences

other people concerned. Serious assault on or abuse or neglect of a child should be reported so that officers can investigate and consider prosecution.

General practitioner—Whether or not concerned directly in the initial investigation the general practitioner has a diagnostic role concerning injuries or a child's health and development and has significant knowledge of the child and family. This will assist the conference in appraising risk and needs.

Hospital doctors are sometimes the first to suspect or identify abuse or neglect. They will advise the conference on diagnosis, and on whether the signs and symptoms observed are attributable to care given by parents or carers to the child.

Health visitors, school nurse, and nurse managers contribute knowledge of the child and family and sometimes the general practitioner's information and opinions. They may contribute to the child protection plan, especially when this entails monitoring a child's health and development. The nurse manager provides support and represents this part of community health services.

Probation officer—He or she may be working with family members or able to provide information about previous or possible involvement with the family (for example, work with offenders or marital work).

Voluntary organisations may be involved where they provide or could offer services to children and families.

Armed services are involved where cases have a service connection.

The circumstances of the case may indicate the involvement of other agencies or professionals: the local authority housing department, especially when there are rent arrears, overcrowding, or questions of homelessness; the Department of Social Security, where financial difficulties are significant; clinical medical officers and doctors working in the community—for instance, in schools—who are well placed to detect signs and symptoms of abuse or neglect; psychiatrists and members of community mental handicap teams; and hospital nursing staff.

Case conferences must have available specialist advice: a lawyer from the local authority's legal section; a psychiatrist, and psychologist or paediatrician, or both; and interpreters and specialists working with disabled people and people from minority ethnic groups. Their role is to contribute to informed decision making—for example, about legal options; the significance and treatment of medical symptoms and signs; and the cultural components to a case.

Once a court has granted an emergency protection or interim care order and appointed a guardian *ad litem*, this officer of the court, whose role is to advise the court on issues of case management, to represent the interests of the child, and to provide courts with an independent social work perspective, may attend as an observer.

General practitioners and hospital doctors may claim a fee for attendance at case conference.

Parental attendance

Parents and children must be invited to attend case conferences unless the chairperson decides that their exclusion is justified—for the child because of their age and understanding; for parents where attendance would preclude proper consideration of the child's interests. This includes the likelihood of the conference being disrupted, violence towards professionals or the child, or undue influence being exerted by parents on a child. It does not include the possibility of prosecution. The reasons for exclusion should be recorded in the child's file.

Where the interests of parents and children conflict the child's interests have priority. If parents and children are not present the conference must receive or ask for a report of their views (a written report, statement, or audio tape) and ensure that they receive detail of the discussion and recommendations.

Local child protection procedures, agreed by area child protection committees, will detail how parental and child attendance, ideally for the entire conference (although separate attendance may be necessary) should be facilitated. Including parents and children exemplifies the Children Act's commitment to partnership and requires professionals to address envisaged problems, such as sharing confidential information, through training and procedural preparations.

Meaningful family participation can be facilitated by the following:

(1) Partnership underpinning all work with the family—openness, consultation, and consideration of wishes and views expressed.

(2) Leaflets explaining the nature and purpose of case conferences.

(3) Training for professionals.

(4) Preparatory work with children and parents on their contribution to case conferences.

(5) Assistance to facilitate attendance—for example, timing, venue, fares, and creche facilities.

(6) Enabling parents and children to bring an advocate to support and advise them.

(7) Written reports from professionals which distinguish facts and observations from opinion.

(8) Active chairing—introducing the participants, clarifying purposes, and ensuring language is "client friendly."

(9) Open discussion about the nature and degree of risks and the resources required, including those from the family, to implement the recommended plan.

(10) Provision of minutes and written notification of decisions and recommendations, with follow up to clarify any outstanding issues

Child protection review

These meetings agree the child protection plan after a comprehensive assessment or review the plan, making changes where necessary, by considering current risks and needs in the family and whether the plan continues to protect the child. They review interagency cooperation and consider if registration should be continued or terminated. The usual interval between these reviews will be at least six months, but anyone may request a review at any time. Once the child protection plan has been agreed a core group of professionals will be identified as key, essential contributors to these reviews. The same requirements concerning parental and child attendance apply here.

Statutory reviews

When children are being looked after by the local authority statutory reviews are required after the first four weeks, three months, and every six months thereafter. They may be combined with child protection reviews. Parents and children are invited to attend, separately when this is indicated, with an officer of the social services department (not the social worker or team leader) responsible for coordinating the review and reports, including annual health reports. The local authority is required to consult and consider the views of the child, parents, and other people relevant to the case, including health care professionals. The child's views about the attendance of professionals at these reviews must be considered. Each review must reappraise the plan for the child, including case objectives, any variations to the child's placement, legal status, contact with family, and education and health needs. A formal record is made of the review, and the results sent to those concerned in the case.

Area child protection committees

The role of area child protection committees may be described as follows:

(1) To determine and review arrangements for working together—developing clear policies on roles and responsibilities in prevention, assessment, investigation, and treatment of child abuse and neglect; and publishing these procedures, including the principle of including parents and children at all conferences.

(2) To develop and review joint training—covering assessment, investigation, and treatment; race and gender issues; children with disabilities; how feelings about abuse affect practice; and professional stereotypes.

(3) To encourage and review interagency cooperation.

(4) To develop and review arrangements for expert advice.

(5) To review and where necessary inquire into cases.

(6) To monitor case conferences and the implementation of legal procedures.

(7) To publish an anual report.

The core membership comprises senior officers or professionals, with delegated decision making powers, from the social services department, NSPCC, police, probation service, district health authority, and nursing profession; and representatives from general practice, medicine, and psychiatry; family health services authority; local education authority; armed services (where appropriate); and education. Other agencies which may be involved include voluntary organisations, housing departments, the Department of Social Security, and those with particular expertise, for instance in religious, ethnic, and cultural matters.

The representatives pass reports and recommendations to their own agencies, and inform the area child protection committee of their agency's work in child protection.

Factors necessary for effective child protection meetings

- Shared values and purposes
- Theoretical agreement about child protection issues
- Cooperation based on agreed roles, acceptance and understanding of differences (work focus) and agency structures (decision making), and negotiating overlap of areas of expertise
- Recognising and working with, not avoiding, conflict or difference
- Adequate preparation, consistent membership or attendance, and no key absences. Clarity of decision making responsibility
- Chairperson who focuses the meeting on the task and, when appropriate, enables the meeting to consider group dynamics issues
- Absence of jargon and professional mystique, recognition of anxiety and stress in child protection work, explicit discussion of degrees of risk when appropriate, and willingness to reappraise professional (status and power) and gender stereotypes
- Careful timing of meetings to facilitate attendance
- Adequate recording of discussion, facts, decisions, recommendations, tasks, and interagency plans

Further reading

Bridge Child Care Consultancy Service. *Sukina. An evaluation report of the circumstances leading to her death.* London: BCCCS, 1991.
Corby B, Mills C. Child abuse: risks and resources. *Br J Social Work* 1986;**16**:531–42.
DoH. *Working together under the Children Act 1989. A guide to arrangements for inter-agency co-operation for the protection of children from abuse.* London: HMSO, 1991.
Family Rights Group. *The Children Act 1989—an FRG briefing pack.* London: FRG, 1991.
Jones D, Pickett J, Oates M, Barbor P. *Understanding child abuse.* London: Macmillan, 1987.

PROTECTING CHILDREN

Barbara Mitchels

Child abuse can be physical, sexual, or emotional. Just as forms of abuse vary, so do the needs of each child and family. The Children Act 1989 was described by the Lord Chancellor as ". . . the most comprehensive and far reaching reform of child care law . . . in living memory." The act radically reforms child care law, embodying challenging changes of principle and practice in child protection. It creates a new court of three levels with concurrent jurisdiction comprising the High Court, county court, and magistrates court. Cases can move up or down the levels within the court as necessary, and to avoid delay. Subsidiary legislation, rules, and guidance following the act form a substantial body of reading material (see further reading).

Underlying principles of the Children Act
Non-intervention

The new legislation is designed to encourage negotiation and cooperation between parents, children, and professionals, enabling children to remain within their own families with an appropriate input of resources, rather than removing them to alternative accommodation. The emphasis is on facilitation—empowering parents and families rather than paternalistic control. The act creates several new private and public law orders, giving the court a wide choice of possibilities with which to meet the needs of a child. It also insists that the court shall make no order unless it is better for the child to do so than not making an order at all. In each case the court has to ask itself the question "Do we need to make an order at all?"

Avoidance of delay

The act is based on the principle that delay is not deemed to be in the interests of the child. Courts will be taking a proactive role, controlling timing through "directions hearings" in which the parties, notice, time for filing and service of evidence and reports, and the hearing dates will be agreed. The court needs to know of dates to avoid when an expert is not available to give evidence, in advance of the directions hearing. These hearings are also a forum for discussion and organising of medical and psychiatric examination or assessment with informed consent, and, where appropriate, contact, and other issues relevant to the particular case.

The welfare of the child is of paramount importance

The main principle of the act is that the child's welfare is the paramount consideration for the court. There is a welfare checklist giving a statutory guideline of the issues to which the court must have regard in making decisions about care, supervision, contact, and certain contested private law orders. Whenever reports are written for use in court the welfare checklist should be borne in mind, even when it is not compulsory to do so. It is a very useful guide to the court's thinking. One of our leading judges said recently that "The child is a person, not an object of concern." Clearly, a child cannot always know what is best for him or her, therefore his or her wish cannot be the sole basis for the court's decision, but the wishes and feelings of the

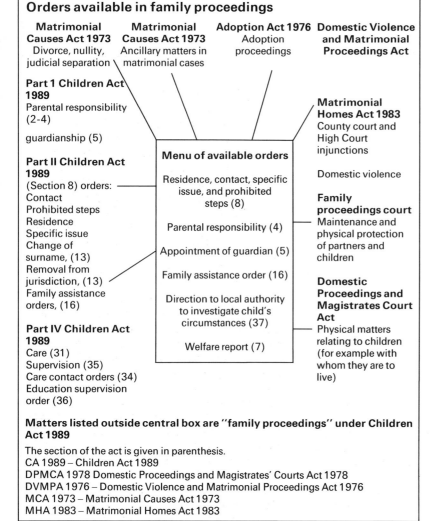

Orders available in family proceedings

Matrimonial Causes Act 1973
Divorce, nullity, judicial separation

Matrimonial Causes Act 1973
Ancillary matters in matrimonial cases

Adoption Act 1976
Adoption proceedings

Domestic Violence and Matrimonial Proceedings Act

Part 1 Children Act 1989
Parental responsibility (2-4)

guardianship (5)

Part II Children Act 1989
(Section 8) orders:
Contact
Prohibited steps
Residence
Specific issue
Change of surname, (13)
Removal from jurisdiction, (13)
Family assistance orders, (16)

Part IV Children Act 1989
Care (31)
Supervision (35)
Care contact orders (34)
Education supervision order (36)

Menu of available orders

Residence, contact, specific issue, and prohibited steps (8)

Parental responsibility (4)

Appointment of guardian (5)

Family assistance order (16)

Direction to local authority to investigate child's circumstances (37)

Welfare report (7)

Matrimonial Homes Act 1983
County court and High Court injunctions

Domestic violence

Family proceedings court
Maintenance and physical protection of partners and children

Domestic Proceedings and Magistrates Court Act
Physical matters relating to children (for example with whom they are to live)

Matters listed outside central box are "family proceedings" under Children Act 1989

The section of the act is given in parenthesis.
CA 1989 – Children Act 1989
DPMCA 1978 Domestic Proceedings and Magistrates' Courts Act 1978
DVMPA 1976 – Domestic Violence and Matrimonial Proceedings Act 1976
MCA 1973 – Matrimonial Causes Act 1973
MHA 1983 – Matrimonial Homes Act 1983

Legal procedures to protect children

First negotiate and try to agree solution with the family and child
Could the child stay within the family with input of resources?
If negotiation fails, then a court order or police action may be necessary

Sequences of action

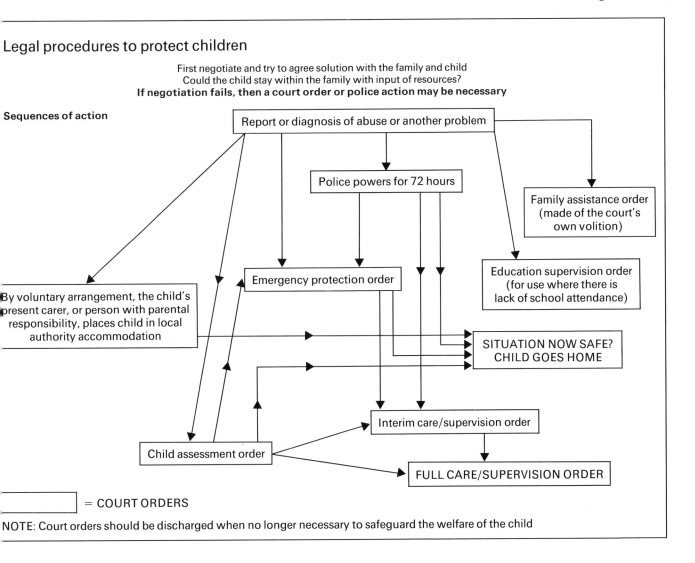

☐ = COURT ORDERS

NOTE: Court orders should be discharged when no longer necessary to safeguard the welfare of the child

child should be ascertained and taken seriously. Even very young children can indicate feelings by non-verbal means, but skill is required in interpretation. One of the tasks of the court welfare officer and the guardian *ad litem*, assisted whenever necessary by expert evidence, is to advise the court of the child's wishes and feelings.

Welfare checklist

(1) The ascertainable wishes and feelings of the child concerned (considered in the light of his age and understanding).

(2) The child's physical, emotional, and educational needs.

(3) The likely effect on the child of any change in his or her circumstances.

(4) The child's age, sex, background, and any characteristics which the court considers relevant.

(5) Any harm that the child has suffered or is at risk of suffering.

(6) How capable each of the parents, and any other person in relation to whom the court considers the question to be relevant, is of meeting the child's needs.

(7) The range of powers available to the court under this act in the proceedings in question.

Parental responsibility

On 14 October 1991 the legal relationship between all parents and their children changed. The act creates the new concept of parental responsibility, defined as "all the rights, duties, powers, responsibilities and authority which by law the parent of a child has in relation to a child and his property." However, not all parents now have parental responsibility for their children; the act creates several categories. Parents married to each other at the time of their child's birth or subsequently, and every mother of a child born to her (married or not) automatically acquire parental responsibility for their child, which will be lost only by adoption. Natural fathers may acquire parental responsibility by written agreement with the mother in a format laid down in a statutory instrument (No 1478 of 1991) signed by both parties, then registered at Somerset House. Copies may be obtained for a £5 fee, in the same way as a birth certificate. Natural fathers may also seek a court order for parental responsibility if the mother does not agree. A court also has power to remove it later. Others may acquire parental responsibility along with court orders such as residence, care, or emergency protection. These are discussed below. More than one person can have and share parental responsibility for a child at the same time.

Parental responsibility is the legal footing for decision making in a child's life; although the act provides that those without it may "do what is reasonable in all the circumstances to safeguard and promote the welfare" of a child in their care: for example, this section 3(5) therefore would enable a babysitter or neighbour to take a child to hospital or the police in an emergency.

Medical examination and assessment of children

A distinction must be made at the outset between examinations and assessments for necessary treatment and those purely to gain evidence for a court.

Treatment of children

In so far as general (non-emergency) treatment is concerned, consent will be required from a person having parental responsibility for a young child, or from the child if he or she is competent to make medical decisions. Such competence depends on age, intelligence, understanding, and the information given. Examinations carried out without such consent could constitute an assault and could render the practitioner liable in civil or criminal law, or both. Where emergency treatment is required the ethical rule applies that practitioners must rely on their own clinical judgment if those in a position to give consent are unavailable. The High Court may in certain circumstances use its inherent or wardship jurisdiction to override those with parental responsibility or the child. Medical consent presents a constant problem for practitioners. There is insufficient space to discuss it fully here, but some of the publications listed at the end of this chapter look at consent issues in greater detail.

Control by the court of examinations for forensic purposes

Repeated medical and psychiatric examinations for forensic purposes can cause a child further unnecessary stress. The act empowers the court in the context of emergency protection orders, child assessment orders, and interim orders for care and supervision, to regulate such examinations and make any appropriate directions, which could include nomination of the practitioner(s) to carry out the examination or assessment, the venue, those to be present, and those to whom the results may be given. Any unauthorised evidence obtained without observing this rule may not be allowed in court.

The child's right of refusal under the Children Act

The child may make an informed decision to refuse an examination or assessment, even if it has been authorised by the court. The decision of the child will depend on his or her age and understanding and whether the information given has been sufficient. Practitioners are advised to ensure that a child capable of understanding is always given an age appropriate explanation of what is to be undertaken. A note should be made both of the information given and of the substance of the questions and answers that give rise to the practitioner's decision about the child's capability to make an informed decision. That note may be later required in court. In care, supervision, or emergency protection proceedings a guardian *ad litem* will have been appointed at an early stage and will assist where necessary. Where a child is brought to the doctor in accordance with a direction of the court, but then refuses, the examination should not proceed, but the matter should be referred back to the court.

Emergency protection order

An emergency protection order may be made where the court has reasonable cause to believe that a child is likely to suffer significant harm unless removed from where he or she is, or kept where he or she is; or the child cannot be seen in circumstances where he or she might be suffering significant harm. It is short: eight days initially, with the possibility of a further extension of seven days only. Anyone may apply for the order, including a doctor, but usually it will be the local authority or the police. It may be granted without notice, and by a single justice. There is no appeal, but after 72 hours it may be challenged in specified circumstances.

The court will appoint a guardian *ad litem* for the child, and give necessary directions—for example, entry and search, disclosure of the child's whereabouts, medical examinations, and contact. Police or doctors may be asked to assist the local authority to execute the order. The applicant gains temporary parental responsibility for the child, who may be looked after away from home in either local authority accommodation or hospital. The child must be returned home as soon as it becomes safe to do so; or if the situation remains unsafe renewal or another protective order must be sought before the emergency protection order expires.

Police powers to remove a child to a safe place or prevent removal from a safe place

Police have their own powers under the act to remove a child to suitable accommodation for 72 hours where there is reasonable cause to believe that the child would otherwise be likely to suffer significant harm. The police may also use their powers to prevent the removal of a child from a safe place such as hospital. In situations where abuse or other significant harm is suspected doctors may need to call on this power where those with parental reponsibility are seeking to remove a child admitted to hospital, or to ensure that a child in need of treatment is taken from a general practice to hospital. The 72 hour duration allows time for further investigation of the

Definitions of the terms used in the Children Act

Harm	Ill treatment or the impairment of health and development
Development	Physical, intellectual, social, emotional, or behavioural development
Health	Physical or mental health
Ill treatment	Includes sexual abuse and forms of ill treatment that are not physical

child's circumstances and for a court order to be sought where necessary.

Care and supervision

There is now only one route for a child to be taken into statutory care—by proving the grounds laid down in section 31 of the act. Care orders are no longer an option in matrimonial or criminal proceedings. They may last until a child reaches 18, or may be discharged earlier on application to the court. Supervision orders may last for one year, with possible extensions for up to one year at a time, to a maximum of three years.

The grounds for care and supervision are the same, and only a local authority or authorised person (currently a member of staff from the NSPCC) may apply. The court must have regard to the welfare checklist, the principles of non-intervention, and avoidance of delay and be satisfied that (a) the child concerned is suffering or likely to suffer significant harm; and (b) that the harm, or likelihood of harm is attributable to either the care being given or likely to be given if an order were not made, not being what it would be reasonable to expect a parent to give; or the child being beyond parental control. The threshold criteria for care and supervision are measured objectively, against a reasonable standard of parenting. Not only must the existence or likelihood of significant harm be found but this must be attributable to the standard of parenting experienced by the child falling below acceptable levels or to the child being beyond parental control. The question of whether harm which turns on health or development is of sufficient degree to be "significant" is measured by comparison to "that which could reasonably be expected of a similar child."

Interim care and supervision orders

Interim orders may last for an initial period of up to eight weeks, followed by extensions of up to four weeks at a time. The timing rules are set out in a rather complex way, but basically, if the first order is less than eight weeks the second must not run beyond the eight week period, and further orders thereafter up to four weeks at a time. If the first order is a full eight weeks then extensions may be up to four weeks at a time. The court is anxious to avoid delay and will be unhappy about continued extensions without very good reason.

Directions for medical and psychiatric examination and assessment

The court has power to order, control, or to forbid medical and psychiatric examinations and assessments when making interim orders. As discussed above, in emergency protection orders the child may make an informed decision to refuse, in which case the matter should be referred back to the court and the advice and help of the guardian *ad litem* sought.

Child assessment orders

The act creates a completely new order in section 43, designed to meet the situation where a local authority has access to a child but there is a lack of cooperation from the child's carers in allowing an assessment to take place. If the child is thought to be at risk of significant harm but in no immediate danger requiring the child's removal or retention in a safe place (for example, a long term, ongoing situation requiring further assessment) then this order may assist. As in care and supervision, only the local authority or an authorised person may apply, and notice must be given to allow parties to make arrangements to attend. The court would have to be satisfied of the risk to the child, and the need for the order, and to be informed of previous unproductive attempts to negotiate with the family. The order may last up to seven days, and the child may go away from home, but this should be only where absolutely necessary for the assessment to take place. On hearing an application for a child assessment order the court may decide instead to make an emergency protection order if it feels that the circumstances disclosed warrant it.

Private law orders

Private law applications are where the issues are between individuals, rather than public law, where the State intervenes in a family's life.

The chart on p 57 shows proceedings designated by the act as "family proceedings," in which the court has power to make the wide range of orders indicated. Some of these, colloquially referred to as "section 8 orders" (residence, contact, specific issue, and prohibited steps), may be made by the court of its own volition. There are certain restrictions on those who may seek an order. Some are entitled to apply, some need leave. A child may, with leave of the court, seek an order—for example, a residence order to live elsewhere, or a specific issue to change school or to have medical treatment.

Since care, supervision, and emergency protection are included in "family proceedings" it will be obvious that in the course of these cases the court has to consider all its options, therefore any expert witness needs to have them in mind, too. The court will need to consider whether to make an order at all and, if so, which would be the best for the child. Any description of private law orders here must be brief, but will give an indication of their effects. The old law of custody, care and control, and access has been replaced with the new (and, it is to be hoped, more logical) concepts of parental responsibility, residence, and contact. A local authority may seek a specific issue or prohibited steps order in the best interests of a child, including a child voluntarily accommodated by them, but not in respect of a child who is in statutory care. It cannot use these orders to obtain care, supervision, or parental reponsibility for a child.

Section 8 orders are defined by the act as follows.

Residence

Residence is defined as "an order settling the arrangements to be made as to the person with whom a child is to live." The order attaches to a person not a place. Residence may be shared—for example, to the mother during term time and to the father in the school holidays. Parental responsibility may be granted to those (such as grandparents) who did not already have it, along with a residence order, and it will run for as long as the order subsists. Special provisions exist for natural fathers. Anyone with a residence order in their favour may take the child out of the country for up to one month for holidays. Otherwise where there is a residence order, removal of the child from the country or a change of surname will require the written consent of all those with parental responsibility or leave of the court.

Contact

Contact is defined as "an order requiring the person with whom a child lives or is to live, to allow the child to visit or stay with the person named in the order, or for the child and that person to have contact with each other." Contact includes telephone calls, tape or video recordings, letters, parcels, and any other form of communication. There is a different contact order under section 34 to regulate contact with a child in statutory care. This has special provisions of its own.

Specific issue

This is "an order giving directions for the purpose of determining a question which has arisen, or which may arise, in connection with any aspect of parental responsibility for a child." This order is designed to sort out disputes between those who want to make decisons about ongoing situations in a child's life and who cannot resolve them by negotiation. It is possible that it may also be used by a local authority, or anyone with leave of the court, to gain a ruling from the court on issues such as medical treatment. Application for specific issue to the High Court could be useful—for example, in a situation where those with parental responsibility for a young child refuse to allow particular treatment, but the medical experts consider this treatment vital in the child's interests.

Prohibited steps

This is "an order that no step which could be taken by a parent in meeting his or her parental responsibility for a child, and which i of a kind specified by the order, shall be taken by any person without the consent of the court." This order is intended to meet particular situations—for example, where a parent is threatening to take a child out of the country without consent. It operates as a preventive measure and may, if necessary, be obtained in emergencies without notice.

Further reading

There are far too many publications following the Children Act 1989 to list comprehensively. Below are a few of those that medica practitioners may find particularly relevant.

Adcock, White, Hollows. *Significant harm*. Significant Publications 1991.

Department of Health. *Protecting children*. London: HMSO, 1988.

Department of Health. *An introductory guide for the NHS to the Children Act 1989*.

Home Office, Department of Health, Department of Education and Science, Welsh Office. *Working together under the Children Act 1989*. London: HMSO, 1991.

Mitchels B, Prince A. *The Children Act and medical practice*. Family Law (Jordans), 1992.

NHS Management Executive. *Consent to examination and treatment*

White, Carr, Lowe. *A guide to the Children Act 1989*. Butterworth 1990.

Introduction to the Children Act 1989. London: HMSO, 1989.

The care of children; principles and practice in regulations and guidance. London: HMSO, 1989.

The Children Act 1989 guidance & regulations Vol 1 Court orders. London: HMSO, 1991.

The flow charts are reproduced from *The Children Act and Medical Practice* with kind permission of Family Law.

MEDICAL REPORTS

Roy Meadow, Barbara Mitchels

Notification

A doctor who is worried that a child has been abused should telephone the head of the local social work department, whether the department is in the hospital, is a community district department, or is in the legal department of the local authority. If the case is urgent action may be required immediately. Always immediately follow up the conversation with a brief letter stating the cause of concern so that there is no chance of it being forgotten. The letter, marked confidential, may be brief but should be written in language understandable to a non-medical person.

Medical reports

Formal reports are required by the courts whenever medical evidence is being used in child abuse cases. Great care must be taken over the construction of the report so that fact and opinion are clear. Sometimes a solicitor will ask you to address particular issues in detail, but quite often the doctor is asked merely for a "medical report."

- The report should be typed in double spacing with wide margins. It is useful to number the paragraphs or sections consecutively so that they can be referred to easily during discussion or in court.
- In Children Act cases the document should be headed
In the . . . . . . court
Case Ref No . . . . . .
Re . . . (name of child, date of birth, age).
In the top right hand corner put
Filed on behalf of . . . .
Statement No . . . .
Date . . . . . .
- Do not give the child's address or any information that would identify foster carers or adoptive parents unless first cleared with the court or the instructing advocate.
- At the start give your full name, current position, and medical qualifications. Follow that with some indication of previous relevant experience—for example, "I have been a principal in general practice for 12 years" or "I am a paediatric registrar who has worked with children for five years." If you have had particular training or experience of child abuse mention its extent; if you have published research work on the subject say so.
- Make clear the nature of your interest in the case in terms of how you came to encounter the child and how long you have been concerned with the case and in what capacity. State the extent of your knowledge of the case in terms of correspondence and discussion with colleagues and the nature of the documents and reports that you have seen. Sometimes many hospital records and documents will have been studied, in which case a statement such as "I have studied the case notes and relevant documents" is sufficient.

- State the extent of your contact with the child—for example, "I examined the child in my outpatient clinic and discussed the problems with the parents. The consultation lasted 50 minutes" or "I assessed the child every month during the following year, each assessment lasting about 15 minutes."
- Summarise the case, being careful to amplify any medical jargon as the report will be read by many non-medical people and will probably be seen by the child's parents. Terms such as petechiae or apnoea need explanation. When relating the clinical history write it down chronologically and in addition to the date make clear the child's age at each incident.
- Clinical findings follow the history and should be set out in an ordered fashion. A diagram or photograph may be added to supplement the description. When the pattern of injury is typical—for example, finger marks showing a firm grip on a child or slap marks—an explanation of how and why that pattern is recognisable is helpful to lay people. Though the main findings may relate to a particular injury or to just one part of the body, always include a general appraisal of the child, including his or her height and weight (and their centile value) and a note on the child's developmental abilities. This should be followed by a note of the child's behaviour during the consultation or at any other times that you have observed the child with the parents or elsewhere.
- The conclusion or opinion should be clear but not too dogmatic. The court wants to know your opinion and if possible to evaluate it. Remarks such as "the findings are compatible with" can be extraordinarily unhelpful, and you should try to give an indicator of likelihood in terms of probability. State the reasons for your opinion in the report and be prepared to discuss them subsequently. Any confirmatory pathological or radiographical findings should be reported, explained, and interpreted.

Medical reports

Report checklist

Name

Practising address

Work Tel No/Fax No

Professional position or appointments held

Qualifications

Relevant experience

Confidentiality checked—authority for child's address to be disclosed?

Welfare checklist—does the report take this into account?

List of people interviewed or consulted in connection with the preparation of this report with appropriate details: times, dates, location, frequency, where relevant

List of places visited in the preparation of the report, with details where relevant

List of samples taken for the preparation of the report, with details if relevant of the times and places the samples were taken

Chronology—can be useful to get things in context

Final check with diary and notes. Are the details of dates and times given in the report accurate?

Does the report refer to quoted comments from any interviews?
If so, is there a contemporaneous note, and is the report giving an accurate account of what the notes record?

If the report is based on information provided by others does the report make clear the nature of the information given, its source, the weight given to it, and the extent to which it has been relied upon? Is there authority for disclosure of sources of information?

Does the report make clear the basis on which opinion is given and conclusions are drawn?

Has jargon been avoided?

Where technical terminology is unavoidable, is it also explained in clear terms?

Is the thinking process in the report clear and well reasoned?

Have all possible alternatives—for example, of diagnosis, treatment, assessment—been explored and evaluated, and is this made clear in the report?

Are there specific legal requirements for this case?
Have they been met?

Are there specific legal requirements of format or content for this court report?
Are they all fulfilled?

List of exhibits referred to in the report . . . and are they attached?

List of refences cited, authorities quoted, or any other work relied on in the report; copies, if appropriate, attached as exhibits, or will they be available for use in court?

- When providing an expert medical opinion in a statement for court, ensure that all known relevant reasons leading to the conclusion and opinions given are included in the original statement and clearly set out. If additional facts or reasons come to light after that statement is filed the court may give leave to file an additional statement. The courts may refuse to admit evidence of matters not contained in a statement filed with the court, since the other parties will not have had a chance to consider or refute whatever is being postulated.
- If you have seen a statement from another party that contradicts your opinion finish your statement by making clear which of your findings are consistent with the contradictory statement and which are not, making any relevant comments arising from those contradictions.
- The Children Act rules require that statements for court carry at the end the following:

> "I . . . (full name) . . . declare that the content of this statement is true to the best of my knowledge, information and belief, and I understand that it may be placed before the court."

Reports for criminal proceedings have their own format, on the requirements of which the Crown Prosecution Service will advise.

- Expert witnesses have additional roles. The duty of the expert may include an explanation of child development, child behaviour, and the effect of adverse factors such as abuse on the child. Thus the expert is drawing attention to the particular needs of the child for the benefit of those who have less experience with children. The expert witness may sit through the hearing to advise upon the different evidence presented. He or she may also be asked before the hearing to assess all the evidence and interview the family in order to present an authoritative opinion at the hearing.

Police reports

In some cases of child abuse the police will ask for a report in the form of a witness statement. This needs to be on a police reporting form, which is available from either the local police station or the police officer who has asked for the report. Police officers like to come with their notebooks and write the report themselves and then present it to the doctor to sign. Many doctors do not like this because they find that the report they are asked to sign is written in language that they would not use ("I proceeded to the ward where I ascertained that the minor was in bed and commenced my investigation") or which does not quite reflect the opinion that they want to give (and would give if writing it themselves). Therefore most doctors prefer to write their own police report in the approved format and send it to the police station. Sending the report by post allows more time for necessary thought and preparation. A hastily written report may be harmful to the case and also to the reputation of the expert. Under no circumstances should a doctor give in to pressure from the police or any other agency to prepare a report too hastily. The police officers will make it clear which areas of information they want in the report. Police reports are usually much briefer than the lengthy medical report that may be required for court hearings.

Writing a report for the police does not necessarily mean that a prosecution will follow. Once the police have completed their investigation into alleged criminal offences the file is submitted to the Crown Prosecution Service for consideration of the evidence and for legal advice. When the evidence is sufficient the Crown Prosecution Service will conduct the case on behalf of the police.

The Director of Public Prosecutions has a different function. When certain serious criminal offences are suspected the director has the power to initiate an investigation into the matter and to authorise prosecution in the public interest.

Affidavits

An affidavit is a statement of evidence set out in a standard format that has evolved over many years and is approved by the courts. It has to be sworn, or declared, before a commissioner for oaths or other authorised officer (which includes all solicitors and some court officers); a small fee is payable.

Documents or copies of documents that are relevant to the case may become part of an affidavit as exhibits, and copies may be made for all the parties to the case and for the judge. If an expert is asked to prepare a report for a civil case the report (if it is to be used in evidence) will be put into the form of an affidavit by the solicitor for the party calling the expert witness and disclosed to the other side. The evidence may then be agreed, in which case the witness need not attend the trial and the affidavit can be read. Alternatively the evidence may not be agreed and the witness may be called to court to give oral evidence. Oral evidence of expert witnesses may then be limited to the reports that have been disclosed but not agreed, saving the court's time.

Affidavits are not required in Children Act cases, but are still used in other civil actions in the county court and High Court.

Access to records and reports

The Access to Health Records Act 1990 came into force in 1991, giving rights to individuals in relation to non-computerised records held by health professionals about their physical or mental health. Computerised records are already covered by the Data Protection Act 1984.

The Access to Medical Reports Act 1988 gives qualified rights of access for individuals to medical reports prepared about them for employment or insurance purposes.

Further reading

Black D, Wolkind S, Hendriks JH. *Child psychiatry and the law*. Royal College of Psychiatrists, 1989.
Carson D. *Professionals and the Courts*. Venture Press, 1990.
Gee DJ, Mason KJ. *The courts and the doctor*. Oxford Medical Publications, 1990.
Mitchels B, Prince A. *The Children Act and medical practice*. Family Law (Jordans), 1992.

ABOUT COURTS

Barbara Mitchels, Roy Meadow

Even a fool can ask a question that an expert cannot answer.

DR JOHNSON

In cases of child abuse evidence may be required from doctors in various courts. The police may prosecute the alleged offender. There may be child protection proceedings, or the child's family may seek a court ruling on domestic issues arising from the incident.

Doctors may be called, like anybody else, as ordinary witnesses of fact—for example, when they just happen to see a road accident—but more often they are called to court as professional witnesses in relation to one of their patients, giving evidence of fact and opinion on matters arising from their professional capacity as a doctor.

Sometimes a doctor not previously connected professionally with the case is called in as an expert witness to give an opinion or interpret facts using specialised knowledge and experience. The distinction between a professional and an expert witness is blurred. The courts expect all doctors to use their medical skill fully and to give evidence based on their observations, findings, and research by using reference works, notes, diagrams, and other relevant material if appropriate.

Proceedings under the Children Act 1989

Children Act proceedings are civil and the person applying for an order must satisfy the court of the appropriate grounds on a balance of probabilities—that is, it is "more likely than not" that the events alleged occurred.

The Children Act 1989 creates a new court with three levels—the magistrates' family proceedings court, the family division of the county court, and the High Court. Cases can move up and down the levels as appropriate their gravity and complexity.

County court and High Court cases are tried by judges. Evidence in Children Act cases is given both orally and by statement, or sometimes both ways. If an expert is asked to prepare a report or statement for a Children Act case the report will, where necessary, be put in the required format by the solicitor for the party calling the witness and then be disclosed to other parties in accordance with the court's directions. The evidence may then be agreed, in which case the witness need not attend the full hearing and the statement can be read; if, however, it is not agreed the witness may be called to court to give oral evidence. Oral evidence of expert witnesses may then be limited to issues in the statement requiring elucidation or cross examination, saving the experts' and the court's time.

The main body of child protection work will commence at magistrates' level, with some cases of greater complexity or seriousness moving up to the county court and High Court.

Doctors will appear mainly in the magistrates' court or the crown court in criminal prosecutions. For those who are called to give evidence it helps to know the set up of the courts, how to address those present and a little about the differences in procedure.

Currently most care proceedings take place in the magistrates' family proceedings court. The court room is informally set out. At one end sits a "bench" of three specially trained magistrates (the chairman will be the one sitting in the middle); their clerk, a legally trained adviser, sits in front of them, and in front of him or her are tables or desks for the lawyers concerned with the case, the social workers, the parents, the child, and others. Anyone not directly concerned with the case is

The High Court in the Strand

excluded unless the court gives leave for specific people to be present, having consulted the parties.

Ordinary witnesses have to remain outside the court until their evidence is required as they should not be influenced by the evidence of others. Expert witnesses are an exception to this rule and may sit through the case until their evidence is called and remain in court thereafter if they wish. It is very useful to hear the evidence of other experts, together with the general evidence, to get a clear picture of all the relevant issues. Sit near the instructing advocate (solicitor or barrister) if possible—advocates may need a helpful word of advice as they conduct their case.

As a matter of courtesy silence is observed in court during the proceedings by all who are not actively taking part. The court will take a dim view of whispered conversations at the back, so unless a matter requires urgent discussion it is better to pass a note or go outside to converse. If something needs to be communicated to advocates try to attract their attention unobtrusively and they can, if necessary, ask the court for a short adjournment to deal with it or ask the court to pause for a moment while they take instructions.

There are no hard and fast rules as to whom professional or expert witnesses may speak before the case. Doctors may wish to confer with each other, and they can usually do so easily, but it is courteous to confer in the presence of the respective instructing advocates. It also shows the parties to the case who may be feeling vulnerable that they are not being "stitched up" by the experts. If speaking to a non-medical witness is absolutely necessary to ascertain some vital information it should be done through, or in the presence of, the appropriate advocates as there must be no question of possible influence being brought to bear by anyone on another's evidence.

During the case it is wise to consult your advocate about the propriety of discussions with another witness or party. In general, once you have begun to give evidence you should not discuss the case with anyone else.

In civil cases the court has to find the case proven on a balance of probabilities. Rules exist about the evidence that may be produced to satisfy the burden of proof. The most tricky to deal with is "the hearsay rule," which prevents witnesses giving evidence about any event that did not occur in their presence and also (with some exceptions) from relating to the court anything that was said by another person to them. In civil cases (including Children Act and adoption cases) any evidence given in connection with the upbringing, maintenance, or welfare of a child is admissible, even if it is "hearsay."

A doctor may give evidence of facts noted in medical records, even if recorded by colleagues, provided that the notes were part of a "continuous medical record." The original must be available for the court to see if necessary. Amendments should not obscure the original wording but leave it and the amended wording clear, also indicating who made the alteration, the date, and, where appropriate, the reason for the alteration.

Criminal proceedings

Criminal cases are tried in the juvenile courts, magistrates' courts, or crown court.

Appeals are heard in the crown court by way of a retrial, or in the divisional court of the High Court by way of case stated—that is, without hearing the live evidence again.

Appeals from a trial at the crown court pass usually to the Court of Appeal (criminal division) and then on a point of law of public importance to the House of Lords.

In criminal prosecutions resulting from alleged child abuse doctors will be called mainly before the magistrates' or crown court. The burden of proof in criminal trials is to satisfy the court beyond reasonable doubt that the accused is guilty of the crime alleged. As the accused's liberty and reputation are probably at stake the standard of proof is higher and the rules of evidence are therefore different. The Police and Criminal Evidence Act 1984 governs the procedures for interviewing suspects, the taking of intimate samples from suspects, and much of the preparation and presentation of evidence in court. Unlawfully gained evidence may be excluded.

Doctors may therefore find themselves in court giving evidence about examination of either a victim or a suspect, and it is important to remember that the conditions for each are different. Medical or psychiatric examinations of a child for evidential purposes is controlled under the Children Act by the court. The child has a right to give informed refusal under the act (see the chapter on Protecting Children). Examination of a suspect must be in accordance with the provisions of the Police and Criminal Evidence Act 1984.

In the magistrates' court the layout of the

court room and the bench is similar to that described for the family proceedings court, but more formal. The accused will be in a dock, possibly guarded, and the court room will usually have specific areas in which advocates, the public, the police, and others in the case will sit during the proceedings.

The public is allowed into court and the press present may report the case, with safeguards, provided that the child's identity is not disclosed.

Crown court prosecutions

Criminal prosecutions in the crown court follow similar rules of evidence to those outlined above for trials in magistrates' courts. The trial will, however, take one or two possible forms. If the plea is guilty the hearing will be before a judge, whose task is to hear the facts of the case outlined by the prosecution, also the mitigation for the accused, and to sentence the offender after considering the circumstances of the offender and of the offence, together with any reports presented to the court. If it is a contested case the judge will sit with a jury. The jury will be the arbiters of fact in the case, and the role of the judge is to advise the jury on matters of law and evidence and to sentence the offender if he or she is found guilty, again after full consideration of the circumstances and available reports. Sentence may be delayed to obtain any further relevant reports required.

When the trial is by jury the court may seem rather theatrical to witnesses and onlookers. The images of Rumpole or Marshall Hall may affect behaviour and attitudes unless carefully watched. It is tempting to want to impress the 12 people in the jury box with your knowledge, personality, or persuasive speeches, and their rapt attention to the evidence is flattering. But bear in mind that they are people who are doing their best to understand the issues in the case and that they need a clear and concise explanation of the facts and opinions given. They are unlikely to be impressed for very long by meaningless waffle. The judge certainly will not be impressed at all and may well intervene if a medical witness seems to be going off the point.

The waiting rooms in crown courts are often better than those in the magistrates' courts, and there is usually a canteen to keep witnesses going during the seemingly eternal wait to be called. Crown court trials are often lengthy, and the court may be less willing to make special allowances for expert witnesses to get away quickly, although most do their best to accommodate doctors, knowing that they have many pressing demands on their time.

Telephones are usually available for public use.

Be well prepared for court, making sure that the advocate has copies of diagrams, documents, or reports to be used in evidence for the judge, clerk, and the jury, as well as

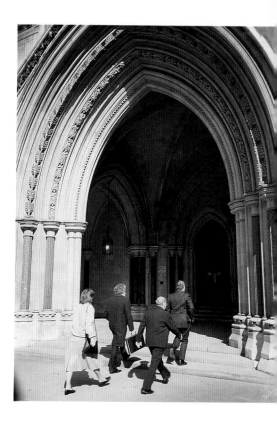

for the advocates and the parties to the case. Medical records and clinical notes are not usually copied, for obvious reasons. Though they may be needed for the doctor's own reference, they would not usually be handed over to anyone else, unless the judge gives a specific direction.

Going to court

Many doctors ask if they have to go to court if asked to do so. In a criminal trial if any person is in possession of facts that are material to the case to be heard before the court, and the court is persuaded that their evidence is both relevant to the issues and vital to the case, the court may order the person to attend as a witness. The court may issue a witness summons, which requires the person named in it to attend the trial. The person summoned is answerable to the court for failing to attend and a penalty may be imposed for not attending. The county court and High Court also have the power to issue a witness summons (subpoena) and order the person to produce relevant documents to the court (subpoena duces tecum). Penalties may be imposed for disobeying the order.

When the evidence is opinion based on observations after an event—for example, the findings on interview of a suspect by a clinical psychologist after an alleged confession to a serious crime—the question arises whether the expert may be forced to come to court and in what circumstances. An expert could be called in by the defence in the course of preparation of a case and prepare a report that proves unfavourable to the defence case. At this stage the defence may decide not to call that witness. It may choose to have the witness in court to assist in the conduct of the case, possibly by suggesting questions in cross examination, but not to ask that expert witness to give evidence. There is no duty to disclose an unfavourable report to the prosecution. But note that section 81 of the Police and Criminal Evidence Act 1984 enables the crown court to require either party to disclose to the other any expert evidence to be adduced in the proceedings. Any such evidence not so disclosed may not be adduced without the leave of the court. In Children Act cases all evidence to be used in court should be disclosed beforehand.

Giving evidence

It is usual to stand when giving evidence but you may be asked whether you wish to sit. In crown and county courts, by tradition, advocates rarely sit, and as it is easier to communicate with someone who is in the same posture as you, standing at ease but not easy is probably best.

In the magistrates' court replies to questions from an advocate should be directed not to the advocate but to the bench, addressing responses to the chairman. In county courts or the High Court speak to the judge when responding to questions, turning towards the judge in order to do so. This discourages interruptions from advocates.

Do not be rushed, and be prepared to refer to your notes or medical records before answering a question.

Any relevant notes, diagrams, and photographs or radiographs may be referred to in giving evidence. If notes—for example, in medical records—have been made by someone else they may be used if they form part of a continuous record and were made by people who have no personal interest in the case. If photographs or radiographs are challenged the advocate may need to call the person who took them to produce them formally in evidence. Charts, reference works, and tables may be used if necessary.

Aim to be concise and clear. Speak loudly enough for everyone to hear and slowly enough for the stenographer or judge to take notes. It is better to speak too slowly than too fast. It is better to speak too loudly than too softly.

Keep your answers brief and do not volunteer long explanations unless asked for them.

Dress neatly and soberly. Behave with dignity (not pomposity); be courteous but not ingratiating.

Do not give opinions on subjects on which you do not have the relevant information or experience.

Occasionally you may have to put up with sarcasm, simulated anger, and obtuseness from an advocate, but keep cool and keep your answers accurate and pertinent.

If an advocate starts quoting a contradictory opinion from a medical textbook and asks if you have heard of that textbook (or scientific paper) ask to be allowed to study the piece, particularly its context, before answering the question. If necessary the court will adjourn to allow you to do so. The advocate will rarely know the subject well enough to understand what is truly relevant, but the witness should carefully consider the advocate's point before explaining whether the question or piece of information is relevant to the matter in hand. Bear in mind that some advocates during cross examination present a barrage of questions and comments that are not always the result of detailed and relevant research but are merely provocative ammunition. There is no need to be upset by the welter of material; simply consider every question and dispose of each one appropriately.

If you do not know the answer to a question say without embarassment "I do not know" or "No." There is no need to make excuses for yourself unless you are asked for them. Being in court is rather like the viva in an examination. It pays to listen carefully to the question and to answer only the question. Put first things first and do not bring in extraneous matter or subjects about which you know little.

As a medical witness your role is to serve neither the prosecution nor the defence but the court. When the court is considering child abuse your duty is to the welfare of the child. On this basis a doctor should be above any partisan feelings and not influenced by any matter other than the best interests of the child. All questions should be answered with this in mind.

Expert witnesses have additional roles. The duty of the expert may include explaining child development, child behaviour, and the effect of adverse factors such as abuse on a child. Thus the expert is drawing attention to the particular needs of the child for the benefit of those who have less experience with children.

As with all speaking engagements, first and last impressions count. Therefore, remember that at the start everyone will be watching and

---

Forms of address in court

- **My Lord or My Lady**: Lords of Appeal (sitting in the House of Lords); Lords Justices (sitting in the Court of Appeal); High Court judges or any deputy sitting as a High Court judge; and all judges sitting at the Central Criminal Court (the "Old Bailey")

- **Your Honour**: all circuit or district judges sitting in the crown court or the county court; and most other judges in the Commonwealth or United States

- **Sir** or **Madam**, or less commonly now, **Your Worship**: magistrates

It is customary to stand and bow to magistrates or judges when they enter or leave the courtroom. Similarly, when you enter or leave a court that is in session a modest bow to the bench or judge is appropriate.

listening to you and similarly at the end when you leave the witness box. Make a good exit, picking up your notes efficiently before bowing to the judge or magistrate. Expert witnesses may wish to remain to the end of the case, but if not the court will usually release them promptly. If the advocate has not asked for you to be excused from the court ask the court "May I be released? I can be reached by telephone and return if the court wishes."

In efforts to be fair to all parties court proceedings are subject to many adjournments and delays. The court officers are, however, considerate of doctors' time and make every effort to call their evidence as soon as possible.

When asked to attend court it is useful to have a diary available and to specify particular times or days when it is difficult to attend because of clinical commitments.

The British Medical Association produces for its members a leaflet (No 33) which provides guidance on legal fees and allowances.

Anyone interested in sharing expertise among the legal, scientific, and medical professions may wish to contact the membership secretaries of the following societies.

● British Academy of Forensic Sciences: The Secretariat, Department of Anaesthesia, The London Hospital Royal, London E1 2AD (071 377 7076)

● Forensic Science Society: Clarke House, 18A Mount Parade, Harrogate, North Yorkshire HG1 1BX (0423 506068)

● Medico Legal Society: Miss E Pygott, c/o Barlo Lyde & Gilbert, Beaufort House, 15 St Botolph Street, London EC3A 7NJ (071 247 2277).

ABUSE: THE EXPERIENCE

Within every type of child abuse there is a spectrum of severity. The severity depends not only on the duration, intensity, and context of the abuse but also on the way in which the family and the professionals deal with it.

The first set of abstracts have been compiled by Sylvia Fraser from her book in which she tells a story which is common. For many years she thought that she was an ordinary person until incestuous memories returned, at which stage she feared she was a freak. Her recognition that sexual abuse within the family is common was, in a strange way, a comfort; she realised that she was still an ordinary person. She makes clear that the denial in her family was a reflection of the denial in the society that bred us all.

Towards the other end of the spectrum is someone else's experience, recounted with clarity and intensity 50 years after it happened—on the beach.—RM

My Father's House—Sylvia Fraser

My father's house was a three storey, frame building on a shady street in Hamilton, Ontario. Though our family found it hard to grow grass because of maple roots, our lawn was always neatly trimmed, our leaves raked, and our snow shovelled. No one drank in my father's house, no one smoked, and no one took the Lord's name in vain. Though my father worked on shifts at the Steel Company of Canada, he always wore a white shirt, navy suit, and tie to his job as a steel inspector—trace memory of a family that had once been prosperous. I was born into my father's house on March 8, 1935 . . . .

I sit on my daddy's lap playing tick tack toe under the glare of a fringed and faded lamp. I have the Xs, he has the Os. I get three across: "I'm the winner!"

There's not much room on my daddy's lap because of his big tummy, held up by a black belt. His tummy feels warm against my cheek. The buttons on his shirt are pearly in the light. I run my fingers down them singing: "Tinker, tailor, soldier, sailor."

My sister, Helen, who is four years older, says: "When you run out of buttons that's the man you have to marry!"

Twice every Sunday my family drives to St James's United Church in my daddy's secondhand Ford-with-a-running-board. I wear white stockings and carry my Dionne Quintuplet handkerchief with a nickel tied in one corner. That is for the collection. My father and three other gentlemen carry the silver plates tramp tramp tramp up to the altar where Reverend Thwaite blesses them, "Thank you, Fatherrr, forrr yourrr bountiful blessings." He means God.

We drive home past the statue of Queen Victoria with a bird's nest on her head and the 16 storey Pigott building, which I know to be the tallest in the world, with my daddy honking every time we get stuck behind a belt-line streetcar. At the foot of Wentworth Street he points to a pile of weathered boards on the side of the Mountain. "That's where the old incline used to run."

I know by now he means a cable car that once ran on a track to the top. Pressing my face against the glass, I stare at this heap of boards, buried in undergrowth. Try as I do, I can make no connection between what I see and the wonder in my daddy's voice. Yet his reverence for things that once were and can never be again inspires my favourite name, the one I use to baptise my oldest and dearest friend: Teddybear Umcline.

Down down down the stairs I go, dragging Teddy Umcline by one ear. My daddy sits framed in his doorway in trousers and undershirt. As I scuff my running shoe over the brass strip marking the threshold, he puts out his black shoe, which he has trouble reaching because of his tummy. I get down on my hands and knees to tie his lace. My daddy smells of Lifebuoy soap. He rubs his face against mine. That's a whisker rub. "You're tickling me!"

My daddy plays with my blond hair. "I had curls like that when I was your age." He plays with my belly button and jiggles pennies in his pocket. My daddy squeezes my legs between his knees. I count my pennies, already imagining them to be black balls and red liquorice from the Candy Factory. The breeze through the window smells of lilacs. It blows the curtains inward like Rapunzel's golden hair, giving me goose bumps.

My daddy and I share secrets.

My mother sprinkles my father's starched white shirts with water from a vinegar bottle. She is reciting a story I know ends with a mouse piping: "Gee whillikers, an owl's egg!" I rock on a hamper of freshly washed clothes, pretending to listen but really worrying if I'll be smart in school.

My grade one teacher is Miss Warner, who is like a barrel with no neck and no waist. Arlene Goodfellow says once when Miss Warner was giving the strap her pants fell down to her ankles!

I am the first to learn all the voices of the vowels and to read the adventures of Dick and Jane and Spot and Puff through to the end. In the cloakroom I teach the other kids to tie their shoelaces in a double bow just like my daddy taught me.

My daddy plays with my belly button, my daddy plays with my toes as he did when I was little: "This little piggy, that little piggy . . . ." Now I lie on my daddy's bed, face buried in his feather pillow. I shiver, because the window is open, the lace curtains are blowing, and I haven't any clothes on. My daddy lies beside me in his shorts and undershirt, smelling of talcum. He rubs against me, still hot and wet from his bath. My daddy breathes very loudly, the way he does when he snores, and his belly heaves like the sunfish I saw on the beach at Van Wagners. Something hard pushes up against me, then between my legs and under my belly. It bursts all over me in a sticky stream. I hold my breath, feeling sick like when you spin on a piano stool till the seat falls off. I'm afraid to complain because daddy won't love me won't love me love me.

I cry when my mother puts me to bed. I didn't used to be afraid of the dark but now I know that demons and monsters hide in the cubbyholes by my bed. I'm afraid one will jump out at me, and rub dirty dirty up against me with its wet-ums sticking out. I beg my mother to stay with me but she says, "Such a fuss!"

I have a scary night. My pillow tries to smother me with its dead feathers. When I wake up I am facedown in vomit. It smells like chicken guts.

Desperation makes me bold. At last I say the won't-love-me words: "I'm going to tell my mummy on you!"

My father replaces bribes with threats. "If you do, you'll have to give me back all your toys."

I tote up my losses: my Blondie and Dagwood cutouts, my fairytale colouring book, my crayons! "My mummy gave those things to me. They're mine."

"I paid for them. Everything in this house belongs to me. If you don't behave I've a good mind to throw them into the furnace."

I think of my beloved Teddy Umcline, his one good eye melting in the flames. "I don't care! I don't care! I don't care!"

"Shut up! What will the neighbours think? If you don't shut up I'll . . . I'll . . . send you to the place where all bad children go. An orphanage where they lock up bad children

whose parents don't want them any more."

"My mother won't let you!"

"Your mother will do what I say. Then you'll be spanked every night and get only bread and water."

That shuts me up for quite a while, but eventually I dare to see this, too, as a game for which there is an answer: "I don't care. I'll run away!"

My father needs a permanent seal for my lips, one that will murder all defiance. "If you say once more that you're going to tell I'm sending that cat of yours to the pound for gassing!"

"I'll . . . I'll . . . I'll . . ."

The air swooshes out of me as if I have been punched. My heart is broken. My resistance is broken. Smoky's life is in my hands. This is no longer a game, however desperate. Our bargain is sealed in blood.

I lie on my stomach on the living room rug, colouring in my fairytale book. I colour the hair of all the princesses with my yellow crayon—Cinderella and Sleeping Beauty and Rapunzel.

My father sits in his fetch-me chair working a crossword puzzle. His pencil snaps. He grunts: "Fetch me a paring knife."

I colour Cinderella's eyes blue, then turn the page to Sleeping Beauty.

"I'm talking to you!"

I colour Sleeping Beauty's eyes blue.

The floor trembles under my tummy. "Fetch me a paring knife."

I shuffle to the kitchen, s-t-r-e-t-ching the seconds like a rubber band, enjoying the terrible tension while wondering when it will snap. I hand my father the knife with the blade toward him, then return to my spot on the floor. With a black crayon, I outline the naked bodies of Cinderella and Sleeping Beauty and Rapunzel, right through their clothes, repeating ME ME ME. Then MINE MINE MINE.

Staring at my father's black boot, I boldly form the thought: I hate you . . . God does not strike me dead. I do not turn to stone. I repeat: hate hate hate hate hate, enjoying the sharp taste of the word like a lozenge in my mouth.

My arms stick to my sides, my legs dangle like worms as my daddy forces me back against his bed. I love my daddy. I hate my daddy. Love hate love hate. Daddy won't love me love me hate hate hate. I'm afraid to strike him with my fists. I'm afraid to tell my mummy. I know she loves Helen because she is good, but she doesn't like me because I am dirty dirty. Guilt fear guilt fear fear dirty dirty fear fear fear fear fear fear.

One day I can stand it no longer. I unscrew my head from my body as if it is the lid of a pickle jar. From now on there will be two of me—a child who knows, and a child who dares not know any longer. She will be my daddy's sexual accomplice. Though we will share the same body, I will not know of her existence. I will not experience, or remember, anything she does with daddy, and my loss of memory will be retroactive. I will not remember my daddy ever touching me sexually. I will not remember ever seeing my daddy naked. I will not remember my daddy ever seeing me naked. In future whenever my daddy approaches me sexually I will turn into my other self, and afterwards I will not remember anything that happened. This memory block will last 40 years.

On the Beach and Afterwards

When the midday meal was over my brother and I walked along the beach in front of our house. This was 50 years ago. I was 8 and my brother 7 years old. After walking a quarter of a mile we saw a man sitting by himself at the foot of the beach retaining wall in an angle where steps led down to the sand from the road. The beach was part of a friendly suburban community where people usually greeted each other whether they knew them or not. So we said hello to this pleasant stranger who gave us a sweet. After some talk he invited us to tickle his chest and abdomen with one of the long pine needles which lay in the sand. I noticed that he didn't have swimming trunks on and had covered his lower abdomen and thighs with a towel. When my brother asked about this he said that he belonged to a group which liked to bathe without any clothing. Soon he moved the towel aside and asked for the pine needles to be brought lower until they stroked his penis. Then he asked where we could go so that we could not be seen.

A few yards away the Home Guard had built a slit trench some eight feet long and six feet deep with boarded sides to stop subsidence, part of the coastal defences. We went over to it and climbed down, concealed from passersby.

In the trench he dropped the towel and asked me to take hold of his now erect penis and rub it. This I did with my brother looking on. He said, "Do it harder," and then, "Do it faster." After a short time white fluid came out and splashed on to the floor of the trench. He then put on his bathing trunks, climbed out, and returned to the beach with us and made us promise not to tell what had happened.

We were excited and puzzled by this novel event and described it to my mother when we got home. She made us soak our hands in disinfectant and said we must not tell my father, but she did so. He questioned us, became silent with a grim look around his mouth as he did when angry, and insisted we go at once and search the beach. When I asked "Why?" he said he was going to thrash the man, adding we were lucky that he had not put his penis up our backsides. My father and I walked the beach without finding the man and then went to the police, which my mother opposed. There we told our story to the village policeman, a dull man with prominent front teeth who wrote it down in long hand in pencil.

My next memory is of walking along a line of men and pointing out the man. Then followed a magistrate's court hearing in a small room when I had to tell the story again, this time in front of the man. I could not look at him. We had promised not to tell anyone and had broken the promise. Then there was a wait of some months until the trial.

For the trial we had the afternoon off school. My father took us to the high court waiting room and left us alone and we had a fight. My brother and I often had fights which I usually won because I was bigger and more aggressive. He hit me hard on the nose and it would not stop bleeding. My appearance in court had to be delayed while attempts were made to stop the bleeding with a cold sponge to my forehead and a key dropped down my back. Then when the bleeding stopped I heard my name being called repeatedly in the way it is in films of courtroom dramas. I was conducted to the courtroom and stood in the witness stand. A man in black in the centre of the room asked my name and then said, "Do you see the accused here?" I replied, "What does accused mean?" Some discussion followed and I was told, "It means the man who is said to have done these things." I looked around the courtroom inspecting I imagine reporters, the public, the jury, the lawyers, and the judge and began to think he was not there. Then I saw him, in the centre of the court surrounded with a rail, pointed, and said, "There he is." I was asked to say what had happened on the beach and then questioned. This was the fifth or sixth time I had gone through the story in an official setting. One question used the name of a different beach as the site of the offence, which I corrected. I wondered subsequently if the wrong name was a test of my lying. My brother then gave evidence and my father took us home.

That in a way was the end of the affair for me, but in another way it was the beginning of a lifelong memory, which from time to time I think through or discuss with a confidant.

In writing this account I have tried to decide what harm I came to as a result of the sexual experience, corruption as the judge stated when sentencing. I have concluded, with possible lack of insight, no harm of consequence. A benefit has been some limited understanding of sexual contact between an adult and child. But the trial, the preparation for it, and the aftermath did cause much worry and helped reinforce the memory so that I am able to write this piece confident in the accuracy of the facts and emotions recalled.

My brother and I shared a bedroom and talked a lot about what had happened. We were worried for some months about the man escaping and coming to look for us to kill or harm us. I have never been aware of feeling ashamed or stigmatised, but did elect to publish this account unsigned. The absence of a sense of shame or stigma resulted partly from the offender being nice to us, partly from my parents, who never made us feel guilty, and partly from the authorities' approach. They tried to ascertain the facts without making a fuss and indirectly conveyed to us that we were not responsible for what had happened.

This absence of responsibility might not be entirely true for it could be said that I colluded to some extent both with the man and with the authorities. My emotion at the time of the act was of intense curiosity and excitement. My brother remembers the same. We had never seen a naked adult man or an erect adult penis. The man had not forced us into stimulating him and we could have left at any time without risk of violence. Subsequently it was probably satisfying to ally myself with the authorities in the pursuit of the wrongdoer with myself as the wronged child, the centre of attention.

The newspaper report of the trial says that verdicts of guilty were returned on eight charges of indecent assault on boys and one charge of committing an indecent act with intent to insult. The judge, awarding a sentence of 12 years' imprisonment, remarked on the corrupting influence on boys and a previous sentence of four years for the same offence. He declared that the man was an habitual criminal and a menace to the community. I do not know what happened to him. He would have been 58 years of age on release from prison after a full sentence.

The abstracts compiled by Sylvia Fraser are from her book, *My father's house—a memoir of incest and of healing* by permission of the publishers, Virago Press.

On the Beach and Afterwards was first published as an anonymous personal view in the *British Medical Journal* 23 November 1991.

Index